C/8

Language A to Z

with David Crystal

cartoons by
Edward McLachlan

LONGMAN

Longman Group UK Limited

*Longman House, Burnt Mill, Harlow, Essex, CM20 2JE, England
and Associated Companies throughout the World.*

© Longman Group UK Limited 1991

First published 1991
ISBN 0 582 07564 5

Set in 11/13 Palatino Roman
Printed and bound in Great Britain by
BPCC Hazells Ltd
Member of BPCC Ltd

To the reader

This is a book of terms which I think are important when you're developing your knowledge about language at Key Stage 4. The book uses the same approach as its Key Stage 3 partner, and has the same title – even though I still haven't got any terms beginning with Z.

Take your time in reading the entries. Several of these entries are longer than those used at Key Stage 3. I often ask you to stop and think, in the middle of an entry. Sometimes I suggest you try something out, as an experiment. I hope you'll manage to do some of these tasks, and if you get some interesting results, keep letting me know.

Once again, my thanks to Ben (third year), Lucy (sixth year), my wife Hilary, and my teacher readers for going through the first draft of these entries, and making so many helpful suggestions. And, as ever, many thanks to Edward McLachlan for adding his unique dimension to these books.

David Crystal

Special symbols

There are four symbols used at various places in this book. This is what they mean.

Don't read this entry until you've read the entry (or entries) mentioned here. If you do, you might have a problem understanding something. I warned you!

Now that you've read this entry, you'll find that these other entries are to do with similar ideas. Have a look at them, if you want to.

This term is explained in the Key Stage 3 book.

There's a related entry in the Key Stage 3 book.

*(as in *Go can I*) This isn't an acceptable sentence in English. People don't say it or write it.

Pronunciation guide

Several entries begin with a guide to the pronunciation of a word. It's always given in brackets. There are two guides given. The first is in round brackets. It shows a respelling of the term, using letters which I hope will give you a clue about how the word should be said. If you're not sure what my letters mean, look in the list below. The second is in square brackets. This is a version of the International Phonetic Alphabet. The symbols used are explained below, too. Several of these symbols are also used in the text of the different entries.

Vowels   IPA

		IPA
a	is the sound of *a* in *cat*	[a]
ah	is the sound of *a* in *father*	[ɑ:]
air	is the sound of *air* in *fair*	[eə]
aw	is the sound of *aw* in *saw*	[ɔ:]
ay	is the sound of *ay* in *say*	[eɪ]
e	is the sound of *e* in *get*	[e]
ee	is the sound of *ee* in *see*	[i:]
eer	is the sound of *ere* in *here*	[ɪə]
er	is the sound of *ir* in *bird*	[ɜ:]
i	is the sound of *i* in *chip*	[ɪ]
ie	is the sound of *ie* in *lie*	[aɪ]
o	is the sound of *o* in *got*	[ɒ]
oh	is the sound of *o* in *phone*	[əʊ]
oo	is the sound of *oo* in *fool*	[u:]
ou	is the sound of *oo* in *book*	[ʊ]
ow	is the sound of *ow* in *how*	[aʊ]
oy	is the sound of *oy* in *boy*	[ɔɪ]
u	is the sound of *u* in *cup*	[ʌ]
uer	is the sound of *ure* in *sure*	[ʊə]
uh	is the sound of *a* in *sofa*	[ə]

Consonants   IPA

		IPA
b	is the sound of *b* in *big*	[b]
ch	is the sound of *ch* in *chip*	[tʃ]
d	is the sound of *d* in *dig*	[d]
dh	is the sound of *th* in *this*	[ð]
f	is the sound of *f* in *fat*	[f]
h	is the sound of *h* in *hot*	[h]
j	is the sound of *j* in *jog*	[dʒ]
k	is the sound of *k* in *kin*	[k]

l	is the sound of *l* in *let*	[l]
g	is the sound of *g* in *go*	[g]
m	is the sound of *m* in *me*	[m]
n	is the sound of of *n* in *no*	[n]
ng	is the sound of *ng* in *sing*	[ŋ]
p	is the sound of *p* in *pen*	[p]
r	is the sound of *r* in *ray*	[r]
s	is the sound of *s* in *so*	[s]
sh	is the sound of *sh* in *ship*	[ʃ]
t	is the sound of *t* in *ten*	[t]
th	is the sound of *th* in *thin*	[θ]
v	is the sound of *v* in *van*	[v]
w	is the sound of *w* in *wet*	[w]
y	is the sound of *y* in *you*	[j]
z	is the sound of *z* in *zoo*	[z]
zh	is the sound of *s* in *fusion*	[ʒ]

When you see letters printed in **bold type**, it means you should say them more loudly, when you're pronouncing the word. In the IPA spelling, the loud syllable is preceded by '. Practise with these:

ladder (**la**-duh) ['ladə]
banana (buh-**nah**-nuh) [bə'nɑ:nə]

a

abstract noun and concrete noun

People usually think of nouns as the names of people, places, or objects you can see or touch – things you can draw or photograph. Think about *handlebars, rabbit, lemonade, London, toenails*, and (you may not know her) *Millicent Twiglet*. These are the **concrete nouns** of the language. But there are many nouns in English which aren't like this, because they refer to ideas, concepts, and other notions that can't be observed or measured. These are the **abstract nouns** – *value, idea, noun, certainty, assistance*, and thousands more. In a book about language, I have to use a large number of abstract nouns. On the other hand, if I were writing a description of a country scene, I'd be using many concrete nouns. So, when you study the style of a piece of writing, keep an eye open for the differences. You'll find that a 'concrete style' (one with lots of concrete nouns in it) reads very differently from an 'abstract style' (one with lots of abstract nouns in it). In the world of newspapers, for instance, the *Sun* prefers concrete nouns, whereas the *Independent* allows more abstract nouns.

But beware! Some nouns can be abstract in one usage and concrete in another. *Music* is abstract in *I adore music*, but in *I've brought my music*, it's concrete. And don't worry if you find some nouns that you can't make up your mind about. *Smell*, in *your sense of smell*, is abstract, but is it still abstract in *There's an awful smell in here*? You can't see it or measure it, but you certainly know it's there. You can argue about this kind of thing for ages – but open the window first!

 noun

active voice see **voice** (in grammar)

affricate (**a**-fri-kuht) [ˈafrɪkət]

Say 'I know the top chop shop' three times quickly! Then, after you've untangled your tongue, say *top, chop*, and *shop* more slowly. The *t* of *top* is one of the plosive consonants. The *sh* of *shop* is one of the fricative consonants. (If I've just lost you, you haven't remembered to check the entries on **plosive** and **fricative** first. You'd better do that straight away.) The *ch* of *chop* sounds like a mixture of the two. And that's exactly what it is. The sound actually starts off like a plosive and ends up like a fricative. This type of consonant is called an **affricate**. The tongue doesn't make a sharp break after the first part of the sound, but moves slowly, so that you hear some friction noise. Say *top*, and you'll hear a nice sharp ending to the *t*. Now say *chop*, and you'll hear a short *sh* sound before you get to the vowel. There are two affricates in English: the *ch* of *chop* is one, and that's written [ʧ] in phonetic spelling. The *j* sound of *job* is the other, and that's written [ʤ] in phonetics. Some words have got two affricates inside them – *church* and *judge*, for instance. I can't think of any with three. Oh yes I can: *Cha-cha-cha*! Or is that a cheat? Can you find a better example?

 consonant; fricative; plosive   phonetic alphabet

agent

Send a message to our agent in China. Tell him we want some results immediately!

I'm not quite sure who said this. It might have been the manager of a factory selling stuffed models of Indiana Jones, or it might have been the head of the British secret service worrying about one of his spies. Whichever it was, one thing is clear: an agent is somebody

who's supposed to get things done. And it's the same when you're studying language. An **agent** is that part of a sentence which tells you who caused or carried out an action. The agent is the 'doer' of the action – and the term **actor** is often used instead. So, who's the agent in this sentence?

Horace ate a banana.

Horace, of course. He carried out the action of eating. And in this one?

The banana was eaten by Horace.

Horace is *still* the agent, even though he isn't mentioned until the end. (If you said *banana*, you were wrong. The poor old banana doesn't carry out the action of eating Horace. This isn't a horror film.) And sometimes you'll find a sentence where there's no agent mentioned at all.

The window's been smashed.

Who smashed it? You've no idea. It wasn't me, anyway.

 voice (in grammar)

alliteration (uh-li-tuh-**ray**-shuhn) [əlitəˈreɪʃn]

Find Fred and Fenella a fresh fizzy fruit juice.
Pop into the park and put the paper in the bin.

I expect you've seen this kind of thing quite a lot. You'll especially see and hear sentences like these in television and poster advertisements. A slogan often has several of its words start with the same sound: it makes the sentence sound punchy and alive, and helps it to stick in your mind, so that you remember the name of the product.

Fishikins! The feline food with the fuller flavour!
Build bigger and better with Bonzo bricks!

When you use words close together which begin with the same consonant, it's called **alliteration**. It's rather like having a rhyme at the *beginning* of a word, instead of at the end. Poets use alliteration a great deal, because it can draw attention to a particular sound effect, or link the meanings of words in a special way. The following are some poetic uses of alliteration. What do you think of them?

3

The barge she sat in, like a burnished throne
Burned on the water

The serpent subtlest beast of all the field

Strong gongs groaning as the guns boom far,
Don John of Austria is going to the war

🪜¹ rhyme   🪜 consonant   🧩 assonance; sound symbolism

allophone (**al**-uh-fohn) [ˈaləfəʊn]

No, this is not something you say in a French accent when you walk into a telephone kiosk. It's an important concept when you're studying the way a language uses sounds. It's all to do with the idea of the **phoneme** (check that you've not forgotten what that is, or else this entry will be as much use as a square tennis ball). You've checked? Fine. Now, tell me a few phonemes in English. Sorry, I can't quite hear. That's right – /l/, /e/, /f/, /s/, and lots of others. Now, look what happens when I study one of these phonemes in a bit more detail. Let's take /s/. You can pronounce this phoneme in several different ways. Stand in front of someone, and get that person to say *see* and *Sue*. (Alternatively, stand in front of a mirror, and do it yourself.) Watch the mouth, to see what happens to the /s/. When the mouth makes the /s/ in *see*, the lips are spread, a bit like a smile. When it makes

the /s/ in *Sue*, the lips are rounded, a bit like a circle. In your mind, it's the 'same' /s/, isn't it, but in actual fact there are two different sounds here – two different ways of pronouncing /s/.

Now it's time for the term. Each kind of /s/ is called an **allophone** of /s/. **Allo** means 'variant of'; **phone** means 'sound'. So the word 'allophone' means 'sound variant'. One variant (allophone) of /s/ has lips spread; another has lips rounded; and so on. Similar kinds of variation are found with all phonemes. Listen to the different ways the phoneme /t/ is pronounced in these words: *tea, too, pot, eighth, stop*. It's quite tricky to hear, but in fact each use of /t/ is slightly different. There are *five* allophones of /t/ here. Can you work out what the differences are?

🪜 consonant; phoneme; rounding

alveolar (al-vee-**oh**-luh) [alviˈəʊlə]

Here's a Mastermind question.

What is the name of the gum ridge behind your upper teeth?

Pass? It's the 'alveolar ridge'. You can feel it easily with the tip of your tongue.

That's the end of the anatomy lesson. Now for the phonetics lesson. If you make a consonant by moving the very front part of your tongue to the alveolar ridge, it's called an **alveolar** consonant. Say *too* and *do*, and feel where your tongue goes as you say them. The [t] and [d] are alveolar consonants, with the tongue making a firm contact at the alveolar ridge. The [n] of *no* is another alveolar sound. Less obviously, so are [s] and [z], as in *Sue* and *zoo*, where the tongue moves very close to the alveolar ridge, but doesn't actually touch it. And if you can roll your *r* with the tip of your tongue, that's another alveolar sound. In the sentence, *Len sat on nine naughty nuisances*, every consonant is an alveolar. Can you make up another sentence which has only alveolars in it? If you do a good job, and someone says you've got 'lovely alveolars', take it as a compliment.

⌗ consonant   ⌂ lateral; nasal; plosive; trill

anacoluthon (a-nuh-kuh-**loo**-thuhn) [anəkəˈluːθən]
plural **anacolutha**

What a mouthful! This isn't a word you'll use very often, I'm sure, but it's a useful one to have around when – Let me start again. An **anacoluthon** is a construction which starts and then goes wrong or fails to finish. I've just used one, as you can see from the dash. The term comes from the Greek word for 'inconsistent'. You won't find anacolutha very often in writing, but they occur a lot in everyday speech. Here's one from a conversation I heard recently, where the speaker gets tangled up in his grammar, and the sentence comes out as a strange mixture of two constructions:

I'm going to a party that I don't know when it will finish.

And here's a transcription of the way one person began a story:

I went – I was walking – When I went to the library . . .

False starts like this are common in speech. But it would be almost impossible, except in a language book, to find a piece of serious prose where the writer started a sentence and then left it so that it wasn't

⌗¹ sentence; syntax

5

analogy (uh-**nal**-uh-jee) [ə'nalədʒi]

'How do you store data on a floppy disk?', I asked a computer whizz-kid one day. He looked sadly at me, as if I'd just come out of the swamp. Then he explained, in a flood of computerspeak. At the end, I said, 'Thank you, but how do you store information on a floppy disk?' He took a deep breath, and tried again. 'Look,' he said. 'Think of a floppy disk as a big circular cake. You cut the cake up into wedges. Each wedge is like an area on the disk, where you can store data.' I began to see what he was getting at.

What's happened here? How was he able to help me, in the end? What he did was 'draw an analogy' between a disk and a cake. An **analogy** is a similarity or parallel between two ideas. Imagine you're faced with a problem which you don't fully understand. Let's call this *Idea A*. You then search for an analogy – let's call this *Idea B*. If it's a good analogy, *Idea B* will help you to understand more about *Idea A*. A cake was quite a good analogy, because I know what a cake is, and I can see how the idea of 'slices' applies to a disk. On the other hand, if he'd said, 'Think of a floppy disk as a collection of petals on a sunflower', I doubt whether this analogy would help me very much. I don't know very much about sunflowers, and I can't see the connection he's trying to make. It doesn't sound to me like a very good analogy, but I might be wrong. I'll think of my stomach and stay with the cake.

anapaest see **foot**

animate and inanimate

Here's a simple task. Find a word from the first column which can go with a word from the second column.

elderly	shop
antique	laughed
the stone	gentleman
the girl	splintered

You shouldn't have had a problem. We don't usually talk about elderly shops or antique gentlemen. Stones don't usually laugh, nor girls splinter.

So what does this show? It shows that you can divide words into two broad types. **Animate** words refer to people, animals, birds,

CAN YOU SPOT THE ANIMATE OBJECT?
Answer at foot of page.

insects – anything that can see, hear, feel, and so on. **Inanimate** words refer to everything else – objects, places, ideas, qualities, and so on. *Girl, doctor, cow,* and *ant* are **animate nouns**. *Laugh, eat, agree,* and *hope* are **animate verbs**, because they're actions that animate nouns perform. *Elderly, busy, careless,* and *foolish* are **animate adjectives**, because they're qualities that animate nouns can have. By contrast, *stone, mud,* and *darkness* are **inanimate nouns**. *Evaporate, congeal,* and *elapse* are **inanimate verbs**. *Global, smoky,* and *molten* are **inanimate adjectives**. The animate sets of words generally go together, and the inanimate ones do. That's why we don't say:

The careless stone laughed.
The busy darkness agreed.
The molten cow elapsed.

Of course, we have to allow for metaphors. Snow thaws, and so does an angry person. And if you're writing poetry, you can say almost anything! In fact, one of the ways poets get some of their best effects is by bringing together animate and inanimate words. *The busy darkness agreed.* Hmm. That's not bad. Feel free to use this line in your next poem. No charge.

GOVERNMENT WORD WARNING! Notice that many words can be used in both contexts. *Grow* is a verb which can be used about anything. People grow. Towns grow. Noises grow louder. Excitement grows. And this entry will grow too big if I don't stop it here.

gender; metaphor; noun

antecedent (an-ti-**see**-dnt) [antiˈsiːdnt]

Geraldine won a radio in the competition, and I won one too.

What did I win? A radio, of course. But how do you know? Because you speak English, and you know that *one* refers back to a noun that's just been mentioned. Linguists would say that *radio* is the **antecedent** of *one*. The term comes from Latin, meaning 'something that goes before', but nowadays it's used in a more general sense. An antecedent is *any* word or phrase which is referred to by a substitute word. It makes no difference whether the antecedent turns up earlier in the sentence or later. It's still doing the same job. You'll see this if I put the two possibilities side by side:

Angelina is a cow, she really is.
She's a real cow, Angelina is.

In the first case, the *she* refers backwards to Angelina. In the second case, it refers forwards. The antecedent is *Angelina*, both times.

pronoun   relative

aphorism (**a**-fuh-ri-zm) [ˈafərɪzm]

The more, the merrier.
Better late than never.
Life is short.
Easy come, easy go.
Unity is strength.

These sentences are all **aphorisms** – short, sharp, wise sayings. An aphorism is a sentence which packs a punch. It makes its point quickly and memorably. Many proverbs take the form of aphorisms. Notice how they often don't have a normal sentence structure: there's no verb in *The more, the merrier*, for instance. In former times, whole books of aphorisms were compiled to introduce readers to a subject, such as medicine or art. These days, aphorisms are used in a more casual manner, dropped into conversations to make a point quickly and concisely. You can have a go at inventing your own aphorisms, if you like. Here's one I just made up:

Language is life.

It doesn't have to be on language. It could be on homework, trains, TV soaps . . . anything.

 proverb epigram

apposition (a-puh-**zi**-shn) [apə'ziʃn]

ME: My friend, Arthur Smirchbucket, has bought a new car.
DRUNK READER: Who did you say has bought a new car (hic)?
ME: My friend has.
DRUNK READER: Beg pargung (hic)?
ME: Arthur Smirchbucket has.
DRUNK READER: So two (hic) people have bought a new car. Your friend and Arthur Whassisname.

Ten out of ten for drunkenness. Nought out of ten for grammar. The two noun phrases in my first sentence obviously refer to the same person, as any sober reader will realise. And whenever you get two nouns or noun phrases placed side by side like this, referring to the same thing, it's called **apposition**. The word comes from Latin, meaning 'to place near'. Here are some other examples of appositional constructions:

Did you see that car, the blue Volvo, just miss the cyclist?
I've just bought a new book, a guide to snake-handling.

9

As a test, try leaving one of the noun phrases out. If you can do this, and you still have a sentence which makes sense, you've got a case of apposition on your hands:

I've just bought a new book.
I've just bought a guide to snake-handling.

But beware! Not every case where two nouns or noun phrases come close together is one of apposition. This isn't, for example:

I'd like you to meet my wife, Arthur.

My wife and *Arthur* are next to each other, but this time I'm talking to someone called Arthur. (You've probably heard of him – Arthur Smirchbucket?) You could take this as apposition only if my wife were called Arthur. And she isn't. She's called Hilary.

 noun; noun phrase

approximant (uh-**prok**-si-muhnt) [ə'prɒksimənt]

Say *yes* very very very slowly, as if you were trying to make up your mind. Like this: *y–y–y–es*. The *y* is a consonant: it goes at the beginning of a word, and it's followed by a vowel. But there's something odd about *y*. It doesn't make the usual kind of noise that consonants make. In fact, if you listen to it carefully, you'd swear that it was a vowel. Its sound is just like that of the vowel *ee*. What on earth can we call a consonant which sounds like a vowel? Some people have suggested the name **semi-vowel**, but a more precise term is **approximant**. Why have phonetics experts cooked up such a mouthful? It's because, when you're making the *y* sound, your tongue moves in the direction of the roof of the mouth, but it doesn't quite get there – in other words, it's 'approximately' there. Are any other consonants made like this? Yes. The *w* sound of *wet* is one. This time, the lips close to make an *oo* sound, just like a vowel, but they don't close enough to make the usual consonant noise. And the way many people say the *r* of *red* is an approximant, too, with the tip of the tongue moving towards the ridge behind the top teeth, but not quite getting there.

GOVERNMENT SOUND WARNING! When you're writing the sounds of *w* and *r* in official phonetic spelling, you can use the same letters: [w], [r]. But when you're writing the sound of *y*, you use a different symbol: [j]. *Yes* is written [jes] and *you* is written [ju:].

 consonant    phonetic alphabet

argot (**ah**-goh) [ˈɑːgəʊ]

THUG 1: Has the dropper got his typewriter?
THUG 2: Right, let's go clean the bowl.

Or, in other words:

THUG 1: Has the assassin got his machine-gun?
THUG 2: Right, let's go get a grave ready.

Thieves, con-artists, murderers, and other members of the underworld often talk like this. It's a very special kind of slang – a secret language which they use as a means of protection – and it's known as **argot** or **cant**. You can see why it's developed. If a casual listener (or a policeman) can't understand what's being said, there's a greater chance of a crime succeeding. I'm afraid I can't tell you very much about argot, for obvious reasons. If I went into a den of crime armed only with my tape recorder, my notebook, and my innocent smile, I don't think I'd get as far as letter B of this book. And I wouldn't recommend you doing any original research yourselves, either! On the other hand, you can look out for examples in crime stories in books or films. And actually, if anything wicked goes on in your school (which heaven forbid!), I wouldn't be surprised if you found some argot on your doorstep.

jargon; slang

So now we know what the expression 'concrete boots' means – Sandy McGill – News at Ten

articulation (ah-tik-yoo-**lay**-shn) [ɑːtikjʊˈleɪʃn]
articulator (ah-**tik**-yoo-lay-tuh) [ɑːˈtikjʊleɪtə]

How do you speak? Do you just open your mouth and it all comes out? Not exactly. It's a much more complicated business, with all your vocal organs working together to produce the range of sounds in your language – and working at great speed, too. It takes only a couple of seconds to say 'It takes only a couple of seconds' – and that sentence contains nearly 25 sounds. The way our vocal organs make sounds is called **articulation**, and any particular part of the vocal organs which helps to make a sound is called an **articulator**. Some articulators move; some

don't. Make the sound [t], as in *too*. You'll feel the tip of your tongue move up to hit just behind your top teeth. It's your tongue that moves. The teeth wait to be hit. So the tongue is called an **active**, moving articulator, and the top teeth are called a **passive**, waiting articulator. Other active articulators are the lips and the lower jaw. And the whole roof of the mouth is one enormous passive articulator.

 vocal organs    consonant; phonetics

aspect

The place – London. The time – the present. Dai Dastardly (Dick's nephew) is hurrying along the wet streets. Every now and then he looks behind him nervously. He stops in a doorway, and stares at the people passing by. He knows that someone is following him. He knows a knife is waiting for him somewhere in the darkness. Dai Dastardly, for the first time in his life, is sweating with fear.

Great stuff, eh? The opening lines of my latest never-to-be-finished crime novel called *Death in the Grammar Class*. But that's another story. Right now, answer me a question. Which tense is the story written in? (Do you remember about tenses? They were in the Key Stage 3 book.) I'll give you the answer, in case it's temporarily escaped your memory. Each verb is in the present tense. I'm writing the action as if it's taking place *now*. But have you noticed that the verbs aren't all constructed in the same way? In fact, there are two types, as you'll see if I put them into lists:

looks	is hurrying
stops	is following
stares	is waiting
knows	is sweating
knows	

The first list has just a single verb form ending in *-s*; the second list uses a form of the verb *to be* (*is*), along with a main verb ending in *-ing*. Why does the story switch from one form to the other? Why not have every verb ending in *-ing*, or every verb ending in *-s*? The answer is that the two forms give you different angles on the action expressed by the verbs. The *is . . . -ing* form emphasises the length of time the action is taking. When I describe Dai as hurrying and sweating, I want to suggest the idea of duration – he's sweating and sweating and sweating. But when he stops, looks, and stares, I'm trying to suggest that the actions take place fairly rapidly. You'll feel this contrast more clearly if I use one verb in both forms:

The train is stopping. (It's taking a while to slow down.)
The train stops. (It comes to a halt, at a particular moment.)

When you change a verb form so that it tells you something different about the passing of time, you are changing the **aspect** of the verb. The *is . . . -ing* construction is called the **progressive** or **continuous** aspect, because it emphasises the idea of duration. The other construction is called the **simple** aspect, because – well, you can't get much simpler than a single verb, can you? Grammar books would describe the verbs in the first column as being in the 'simple present' and those in the second column as being in the 'present progressive' or 'present continuous'.

There are other important contrasts of aspect in English. Here's an interesting one. What's the difference in meaning between these two sentences?

Dai lived in London for years.
Dai has lived in London for years.

In the first sentence, Dai used to live in London, but he doesn't any more. It's all over. This is the 'past tense' of the verb, referring to past time. In the second sentence, Dai still lives in London, doesn't he? The living started in the past, but is carrying on now, and will probably continue into the future. We don't want to call *has lived* a past tense, therefore. There are bits of present and future meaning involved as well. Instead, the *has* form is called the **perfect** aspect of the verb, and it's so interesting I've given it an entry all to itself. If you read it, you'll find out what happened to Dai Dastardly, and learn some more grammar at the same time.

 progressive; tense; verb    perfect; pluperfect

aspiration (a-spi-**ray**-shn) [aspiˈreɪʃn]
aspirated (**a**-spi-ray-tid) [ˈaspireɪtɪd]

What's the main difference between the sounds [p] and [b], as in *pin* and *bin*? Here's an experiment to find out. Put the back of your hand close to your mouth, and say those two words. (Try it now. Never mind if you're sitting on top of a bus or watching *Neighbours*. They're excellent places to practise phonetics.) What do you feel? After the [p] of *pin*, you'll feel a short puff of air. You won't feel one after the [b] of *bin*. This puff of air is called **aspiration**, and it's an important means of telling the difference between several pairs of consonants. We say that [p] is **aspirated**, and [b] is **unaspirated**. Now try doing *too* and *do*, or *coo* and *goo*. You'll find the same effect. See how much aspiration you can get into the aspirated sounds. If it's really strong, you could blow a candle out. But one piece of advice: don't practise strong aspiration with a mouthful of chips. It can take a while to clean up the mess.

 plosive; voice (in phonetics)

assimilation (a-si-mi-**lay**-shn) [asimiˈleɪʃn]
assimilate (a-**si**-mi-layt) [aˈsimileɪt]

Find a friend. Or an enemy. Anyone, as long as they'll cooperate. Get them to say *ten*, and watch their lips at the end of the word. Do the lips close for the [n] sound? No. Now get them to say this sentence, as quickly as they can:

I'll be back in ten minutes.

Watch what happens to the word *ten* this time. The lips will close, and the [n] will sound like a [m]. You can guess why. The next word begins with a [m], and the lips are getting ready to make that sound in good time. When one sound influences another which comes next to it, we call the effect **assimilation**.

Assimilation can work in both directions. In *ten minutes*, the [n] has been changed by the *following* sound. There are lots of cases like this: listen to how the [d] becomes [b] in *good boy*, or the [s] becomes *sh* [ʃ] in *this shop*. Less often, a sound is influenced by what goes *before* it. Try saying *Fish Street*, for instance. The [s] of *Street* would usually come out as *sh* [ʃ]. It's quite difficult *not* to say *shreet*, actually. And sometimes the two sounds influence each other, so that neither sound keeps its identity. Listen to the way some people say *Wotcher doing?* (= 'What (are) you doing?') The middle sound is like the *ch* of *chip*. The two words *what* and *you* have been run together: the [t] sound at the end of *what* and the [j] sound at the beginning of *you* have been fused into a single *ch* sound – written [tʃ] in phonetic spelling.

Seriously, I simply can't stand someone who's so selfish as to assimilate so stupidly sometimes.

Of course, nobody *has* to assimilate. If you want, you can speak slowly and precisely, leaving pauses between words, and ar-ti-cu-la-ting care-ful-ly. Some speakers assimilate very little – radio news-readers, for example. But in everyday speech, we assimilate all the time. And the faster we speak, the more assimilations we use.

♯ consonant; linking sound   🧩 phonetic alphabet

assonance (**a**-suh-nuhns) [ˈasənəns]

Did you ever see the musical, *My Fair Lady*? In it, the phonetics expert, Professor Higgins, is trying to teach the Cockney flower-girl, Eliza Dolittle, to change her accent into one that people consider to be more refined. He gets her to say sentences like these:

How now, brown cow?
The rain in Spain falls mainly on the plain.

You can easily hear how the vowels chime out one after the other. This kind of effect is called **assonance**. The vowel sounds are the

15

same, or very similar, and they have to be in words which come quite close together – otherwise you wouldn't notice the effect. Poets go in for assonance a great deal. Here's an example where *two* patterns of assonance are used at the same time:

So twice five miles of fertile ground
With walls and towers was girdled round

You can hear the [aɪ] sounds in *twice, five, miles,* and *fertile,* and these are blended with the [aʊ] sounds of *ground, towers,* and *round.* Assonance is much less common in other kinds of writing or in speech. I don't think you're liable to find any lines of mine quite so fine.

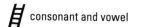 consonant and vowel   rhyme    alliteration; euphony

back see front

bilabial (bie-**lay**-bee-uhl) [baɪˈleɪbiəl]

Bilingual? A person who speaks two languages.
Bilabial? A sound made with two lips.

There are three important **bilabial** consonants in English: [p], as in *peg*; [b], as in *beg*; and [m], as in *Meg*.

I can't think of anything else that it's useful to say just now about bilabials. I can think of something useless to say, though. Two bilabials make a quadrilabial – but you need two people to do it. Work it out.

 consonant; labial

cant (kant, *not* kahnt) see argot

cardinal numeral and ordinal numeral
(**kah**-di-nuhl, **aw**-di-nuhl) [ˈkɑːdinəl, ˈɔːdinəl]

Count from one to ten. (I have a good reason, honestly.) Now do it another way. What way? You know – *first, second, third* . . . We need to be able to talk about the difference between these two ways of counting. *One, two,* and so on are called the **cardinal numerals**. *First, second,* and so on are called the **ordinal numerals**. They work very differently in the language. Compare these pairs of sentences, and you'll see: the first of each pair is fine, but there's something distinctly odd about the second (as signalled by the asterisk).

Two and two are four.
*Second and second are fourth.
It's my 16th birthday today. I'm 16.
*It's my 16 birthday today. I'm 16th.

And NASA controllers don't count down by saying:

*. . . fifth, fourth, third, second, first – lift off!

You can use cardinal and ordinal numerals in the same phrase, if you want:

The first two soldiers were wounded; the second two soldiers weren't.

But beware! Sometimes, changing the order of the words can change the meaning of the sentence:

I've just seen Lucy's two first-floor apartments.
I've just seen Lucy's first two-floor apartment.

(Sorry about this, but linguists love playing with crazy sentences.)

Anything else? Well, you're probably wondering where these rather unusual terms come from (if you weren't before, you don't have much choice now). Both words come from Latin. *Cardinal* means 'principal' or 'chief'. One, two, three . . . are thought to be the basic numbers. *Ordinal* means 'showing a place in a series' – and that's exactly what first, second, third . . . do.

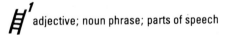 adjective; noun phrase; parts of speech

cleft sentence

Try this out on someone who hasn't read this entry yet. Give them this sentence:

Martha accidentally tore up a five-pound note in the garden.

Now, ask them to make three other sentences out of it, each starting with *It was*. They'll have to do it like this:

It was in the garden that Martha tore up a five-pound note.
It was a five-pound note that Martha tore up in the garden.
It was Martha who tore up a five-pound note in the garden.

In each case, I've chopped the original sentence into two parts, and put one part towards the front. Notice that each part has its own verb (*was* and *tore*). Sentences like these are called **cleft sentences**. What's the point of them? Cleft sentences are a very useful way of changing the emphasis in what you want to say or write. The part that comes to the front is the part that you really want to draw attention to. In speech it's usually the loudest bit of the sentence.

Some cleft sentences are quite famous. Have you ever read this one?

It was the nightingale, and not the lark,
That pierced the fearful hollow of thine ear (Shakespeare, *Romeo and Juliet*)

Notice how using the cleft construction neatly fills out the rhythm of the first line.

So, to make sure you've got the point, try making some cleft sentences out of this next example:

The policeman found the stolen car in the High Street.

It's three cleft sentences you should end up with. All like that one.

 sentence

click

Make the disapproving sounds that are usually written down as *tut tut* or *tsk tsk*. Now make a kissing noise, as if you were telling someone in a mocking way that you loved them. Now do the sound you'd make if you were saying 'gee up' to a horse. Now ask me why I'm asking you to behave in such a ridiculous way.

YOU: Why are you making us behave in such a ridiculous way?

I'm glad you asked me that. It's because I want to draw your attention to the **click** sounds of language. Some languages use clicks as actual consonant sounds – most famously, a number of languages spoken in southern Africa (such as Zulu). English uses them just as occasional noises, and not as consonants at all. They're made in a very different way from the other sounds of speech. English vowels and consonants are all made using air from the lungs; clicks aren't. Clicks are made entirely inside the mouth, using air which the speaker traps between the back of the tongue and the front of the mouth.

You can easily show that the lungs aren't involved in making a click by doing an experiment. Choose a click sound, and pronounce it several times. While you're doing this, you'll be able to breathe in and out without any trouble. Or try this: hold your breath, and make click sounds at the same time. You'll find you can. However, if you try this last idea out, don't hold your breath for too long. I've never heard of anyone clicking themselves to death, but there's always a first time.

consonant; tongue

close vowel and open vowel

Stand in front of a mirror and say these words one after the other:

be bay bear bar

Now try them without the *b*. You'll notice how your mouth gradually gets wider and wider. For the vowel of *be*, [i:], you can hardly see inside the mouth. For the vowel of *bar*, [ɑ:], you can see your tonsils (if you've still got them). 'Say ah', says the doctor, in order to look down your throat – not 'Say ee'! To make an [i:] vowel, the tongue is very high up, close to the roof of the mouth – so [i:] is called a **close vowel** or **high vowel**. Another close vowel in English is [u:], as in *too*. To make an [ɑ:] vowel, the tongue is very low down, with the mouth almost wide open – so [ɑ:] is called an **open vowel** or **low vowel**. Another open vowel in English is [a] as in *hat* – though if you look (or feel) carefully, you'll see (feel) that the mouth isn't quite as wide open as it is for [ɑ:].

And if vowels aren't either close or open? They're between the two, in the middle – **mid vowels**, such as the [e] of bet or the [ɔ:] of saw. And you can make more subtle distinctions, if you want, to show the different heights of the tongue in such words as *bay* and *bear*. You'll have to keep your ears well tuned, though, to catch them all.

‖ consonant and vowel

cluster

In a syllable (remember syllables? check out the entry now, if you don't), you can have a consonant at the beginning and one at the end – as in *rat* and *tan*. But you often get *more* than one consonant at each end, and when this happens, you call the group of consonant sounds or letters a consonant **cluster**. Here are some examples:

rat	tan
*pr*at	ta*nk*
*spr*at	ta*nks*

In speech, you can have up to three consonants at the beginning of a syllable in English, as in *str-ing* and *spr-ay*. [s] is always the first of the three. And you can have up to four consonants at the end: say *glimpsed* slowly–glim-p-s-d (you don't pronounce the *e*, remember). You can have even longer clusters in the written language – for instance, *twelfths* ends with a cluster of five. As you can imagine, clusters of this length are rather uncommon. By contrast, there are hundreds of two-consonant clusters:

glad   dogs   spot   prod   bags   send

And don't forget you can have syllables with clusters at the beginning *and* at the end, as in *sports*, *tricks*, and *stumps*.

GOVERNMENT SOUND WARNING! Don't mix up consonant clusters in speech and consonant clusters in writing. The sounds and the spellings don't always match. *Thumb* has two written consonants at the beginning and two at the end. But in speech there's only one sound at the beginning (see the entry on **dental** to find out what it is) and one at the end. The *b*, as they say, is 'silent'. And beware words like *box*, where there's only one letter at the end, but two sounds – *x* is pronounced [ks].

 consonant; syllable   diphthong

coherence (koh-**heer**-uhns) [kəʊˈhɪərəns]
coherent

We were all looking forward to Saturday because of the match. I've always liked watching Liverpool, though I've never seen them play. Fortunately the bus was late, so we were there in good time and missed the beginning of the game. There was no score until after half-time, when the umpire called 'deuce'.

That's the beginning of Anthony's latest novel. Not bad. Well, not bad for a hamster. But he does have a few points to improve upon. There's nothing wrong with his sentences, mind you. Each sentence is perfectly grammatical, and he's used correctly all the linking words and phrases that join sentences (see the entry on **cohesion** for more about these). But the story just doesn't make sense. It lacks **coherence** – or, to put it the other way round, it's **incoherent**. **Coherence** means that the ideas in a piece of speech or writing all hang together, following each other in a logical or relevant way. You won't find *me* being incoherent in an entry in this book. I take great care to check on that side of things, and I hope you do too. The wallpaper wouldn't be so expensive, otherwise, would it? And the cricket match was cancelled, as a result.

 relevance    discourse    cohesion

cohesion (koh-**hee**-zhn) [kəʊˈhiːʒn]

I thought you'd like to read the beginning of my latest bedtime story for tired teachers:

However, there was a little boy called Fred, and they didn't feel well. She went to get the desk from the other side . . .

I know what you're thinking. Poor DC. It's finally got to him. What a shame. We'll send some flowers.

No need, no need. I am (twitch) perfectly sane. I am just being a linguist, and playing about with the language. To be specific, I'm playing about with **cohesion**. The sentences don't hang together, do they? They aren't **cohesive**. I start off talking about a boy, and the next thing you know I'm saying *they*. You've no idea who the 'they' can be – I've only talked about one person so far. You struggle on, and suddenly *she* turns up. Who on earth is that? Moreover, she

....and then they—who on earth are they – gave it – whatever that is – to her – although who she is, I don't know – she returned it and the other one to him – what other one and who's him and who cares......

went to get *the desk* – which desk? – from *the other side* – the other side of what? And the whole piece begins with a *However*, which suggests I'm in the middle of saying something. You can't *start* a story with *however*!

By contrast, here's a better start:

Once upon a time, there was a little boy called Fred, who lived inside a computer. One day, Fred decided to go and see the queen. However, he didn't know the way . . .

It's quite interesting to go through a piece of writing and find the bits of language which make everything hang together. When you do this, keep an eye open, in particular, for words like these:

meanwhile, he, she, it, they, one, then, this, that, previously, the former, the latter, the following, the above, and so did . . .

GOVERNMENT WORD WARNING! Don't mix up **cohesion** and **coherence**. Cohesion refers to the way particular bits of language link sentences together. Coherence refers to the way the ideas hang together in a logical or expected way. Mind you, if you're not properly cohesive, you won't be coherent either – as my first story shows!

 discourse    coherence

collective noun

You'll know that most nouns have a singular and a plural, and that you form most plurals by adding an *s* to the singular: *boy–boys, girl–girls, horse–horses*. (At least, I hope you know. If not, you'd better sneak a quick look at the entry on **number** in the Key Stage 3 book.) Well, here's a Further Fascinating Fact about nouns. Some nouns have *two* plurals. And one of the plurals looks the same as the singular!

ERIC BLUEBOTTLE: Excuse me.
ME: Yes?
ERIC BLUEBOTTLE: I'd like to give up English and do something easy like nuclear physics, please.

Shame on you, Bluebottle. It's not as weird as it sounds. Let me tell you a story which will make everything clear. Imagine you want to start a new school club. You form a committee. It's a great committee. It meets every Wednesday. One Wednesday the people

Before we start, can we get one thing clear. —Are we a single subject committee, a plural subject Mark I committee or a plural subject Mark 2 committee?

on the committee have a row. They can't make their minds up. They fight and scream at each other. One member is found at the bottom of the river with cement blocks tied to his legs. The *Sun's* headline shrieks:

SCHOOL COMMITTEE TOLD OFF BY HEAD. TWO NEW COMMITTEES TO BE FORMED. Says head: 'The committee are a disgrace to the school. Each surviving member will have extra homework for a month.'

What can we extract from this piece of nonsense? Three uses of the noun *committee*:

The committee was great. *It was* great. (singular subject, singular verb)
The committee were angry. *They were* angry. (plural subject, plural verb)
Two committees were formed. *They were* formed. (another plural subject and verb)

You see? Two plurals. Nouns like this are called **collective nouns**. They have this name because they always refer to collections of people or things. But why have a plural looking like a singular? It's because collective nouns are used in two ways. With a singular verb, you play down the fact that there are lots of individuals involved, and look at the noun as if it were a single unit. With a plural verb, and no *-s* ending on the noun, you do the opposite –

you really emphasise that there are lots of individuals within the group. Try to feel this difference with some other collective nouns:

Our class has maths at 10 o'clock.
Our class are arguing amongst themselves about uniforms.

Their headquarters is to be found just outside Bristol.
Their headquarters consist of several old huts and a garage.

Does that make things clearer, Bluebottle? . . .
Bluebottle? . . .
Where have you gone, Bluebottle?

concord; noun; number, subject; verb

collocation (ko-luh-**kay**-shn) [kolə'keɪʃn]

Let's play Blankety-Blank. Me first. (Well, I'm the author.) You fill the blank.

The house was spick and —.

Did everyone get *span*? I expect so. Still my turn. (You can have yours later.)

When Jemima heard that Emma had won the prize, she was green with —.

What did you suggest this time? *Jealousy? Envy?* There's slightly more choice there, isn't there? (Hey, there's a sentence with three *there*'s in it. I can't remember ever doing that before.) (There, there. Never mind.) Now try this one:

I stuck a stamp on the envelope, and popped it into a —.

What did you get? *Pillar-box? Letter-box?* Probably. But it could have been *shopping bag* or even *puddle*. I know it's not likely, but it's possible! Now try this one:

I saw a —.

Unfair, you howl. You can't fill such a blank. There are too many things you could say.

Are you catching my drift? With some words in the language, you can predict 100 per cent what the following word is going to be (that's *spick and* —). With others you can get fairly close, but it's not 100 per cent. And with others, you can't make any predictions at all. The people who work out the questions in *Blankety-Blank* have quite a task on their hands. They have to find phrases which aren't *too* predictable, otherwise everyone will get them right and there'd be no fun. Equally, they mustn't make them too unpredictable, otherwise nobody would ever agree, and there'd be no fun.

The way words come together in a predictable or noticeable way is called **collocation**. The term comes from Latin words meaning 'to place with'. Word collocations form an important part of the study of vocabulary.

Now it's your —. Make up a sentence, and get a friend to fill in the —.

lexicology

25

comment clause

TEACHER A: Your handwriting is awful.

TEACHER B: Your handwriting, you know, is, to be honest, awful.

Which is the more sympathetic teacher? And how do you know? It's B, of course. You can tell by the extra remarks, which soften the force of what the speaker is saying. Remarks of this kind are often known as **comment clauses**. They're called 'clauses' because their structure is that of a clause – for instance, *you know* has a subject and a verb; *to be honest* has a verb followed by a complement. And they're called 'comment clauses' because they make a comment – a passing remark – on what's being said. You can show this by putting the remarks in brackets, if you like:

Your handwriting (you know) is (to be honest) awful.

Why use them? They're very useful. They tell you the feelings of the speakers towards what they're talking about. And they give speakers a chance to comment on the way they're talking. Here are a few commonly used comment clauses.

I suppose   I must say
I daresay   I'm happy to tell you
they tell me   mind you
it appears   speaking personally

Listen out for comment clauses in the conversations around you. You'll find they're very common, as they're a way of making a conversation run smoothly. But don't overuse comment clauses, otherwise what you say will begin to sound unclear and roundabout, and people will wish you'd get to the point. If, you see, you start, to put it in a nutshell, writing, as it were, sentences with lots of, so to say, comment clauses inside them, you'll find, quite frankly, that your listeners, as a matter of fact, will go, to put it bluntly, nuts.

circumlocution; clause analysis

complex sentence

There's more to this term than meets the eye. If you call a sentence 'complex', you might only mean that it's difficult – containing lots of parts fitting together in complicated ways, like a difficult jigsaw puzzle. Many grammarians, though, use the term in a special way. For them, a **complex sentence** is a sentence containing a main clause, with one or more of its elements *also* being a clause. This sounds complicated, but it isn't really. Just look at this:

Maria dropped the plate yesterday.
She saw a ghost.

Here we have two sentences, each containing one clause. The first clause has four elements in it. (Do you remember about clause elements? I told you about them in the Key Stage 3 book, in the entry on **clause analysis**.) Now look at this:

Maria dropped the plate *when she saw a ghost*.

Do you see what's happened. I've replaced the time-word *yesterday* by the time-clause *when she saw a ghost*. I've had to add the word *when* to link the two original clauses together. And what have I ended up with? It isn't a 'simple' sentence any more, but a 'complex' one.

clause analysis; sentence; subordination   compound sentence

compound sentence

What happened at the party last night? Nothing much. Ted played records. Florence played the piano. David played the fool.

That's one way of telling the story. But it might have been told this way:

Ted played records and Florence played the piano and David played the fool.

Or this way:

Ted played records, Florence played the piano, and David played the fool.

Either way, you've joined all the sentences together into a single sentence, either using *and* as a linking word or the comma as a linking punctuation mark. When a sentence consists of more than one main clause, as here, it's called a **compound sentence**. There are several ways of joining main clauses together like this, but I've only room to give you one last example, using *but* – or perhaps I should use *or* as well, and so round this entry off with a nice long compound sentence using each of the three main linking words in English.

Ħ clause; comma; conjunction; coordination; sentence

concordance (kuhn-**kaw**-dns) [kənˈkɔːdns]

ADA: I'm trying to remember a quotation from Shakespeare. The one about a breach, or going to a breach, or something.
ADAM: Julius Caesar?
ADA: I dunno. Might have been.
ADAM: Macbeth?
ADA: I dunno. Might have been.
ADAM: Hamlet?
ADA: I dunno. Might have been.

This conversation could go on for some time, I suspect, without getting anywhere. How do you sort this kind of thing out? You could try looking in a dictionary of quotations, but if the word you want didn't happen to be part of a famous quotation, you wouldn't find it. What you need is a **concordance** – an alphabetical listing of all the main words in an author's work, showing where they appear. (Concordances don't usually give the **grammatical words**, such as *the* or *of*.) Not all authors have had concordances made of their words, but Shakespeare has. Heave the Shakespeare concordance down from a library shelf, get your breath back, look up *breach*, and it'll tell you *Once more unto the breach, dear friends, once more* (*Henry V*, Act III, scene 1, line 1). Was that the one you had in mind, Ada?

ADA: I dunno. Might have been.

Ħ dictionary; grammatical word; thesaurus

concrete noun see **abstract noun**

conditional clause

TEACHER: If eggs were 60p a dozen, how many would you get for 10p, Blogling?
BLOGLING: None.
TEACHER: None?
BLOGLING: If I had 10p, I'd get a toffee bar.

What do we have here, apart from a developing problem in teacher–pupil relationships? We have, in a word, a **conditional clause**.

BLOGLING: In a word?

All right, awkward, in two words, to be precise – and two conditional clauses. A conditional clause (wait for it!) expresses a condition. You want more?

BLOGLING: Yup.

All right: in a conditional clause, the situation in the main clause depends directly on what is said in the subordinate clause.

BLOGLING: For example?

Well, whether you get a toffee bar depends on whether you have 10p.

BLOGLING: So how do you tell a conditional clause?

Keep an eye open for the word *if*, which is the commonest way of starting one off. *Unless* is quite common, too, and there are a few other words which do the same job.

BLOGLING: Which?

Questions, questions! Look, assuming you've read this entry, and provided you've understood it, and supposing you're on the ball, you'll see that this last sentence has got three more conditional clauses in it. Now go and buy a toffee bar. I really must get on with the entry on consonants.

clause; conjunction; subordination

connotation see **denotation**

consonant (**kon**-suh-nuhnt) [ˈkɒnsənənt]
and vowel (vowl) [vaʊl]

Have you learned to read? If not, you'd better stop here and learn, quickly, otherwise you won't be able to understand the next sentence. In the English alphabet there are 5 vowels (*a, e, i, o, u*) and 21 consonants (all the other letters). All right – you knew that already. But how many consonants and vowels are there in speech? And what's the difference between a consonant and a vowel, anyway?

Seeing as you asked, here's the answer to the first question. In several accents of English, there are 44 – 20 **vowels** and 24 **consonants**. You can hear 22 of the consonants if you listen to the first sound in each of these words: *pin, box, two, dig, king, go, chip, jog, fish, van, thin, though, soon, zoo, ship, hop, mug, no, log, red, wig, yes*. To hear the other two, you have to listen to the end sound in a word like *king*, and the middle sound in a word like *fusion*. You can hear the 20 vowels if you listen to the middle sounds in the next list of words. Don't pay any attention to the way the vowels are spelled, by the way. Just listen to how the words sound: *peep, pip, pet, pat, cup, cart, cot, cord, soot, soon, bird, wait, time, voice, road, house, fierce, scarce, moored* – and the last sound in *sofa*. You may not have all these sounds in your own accent, of course. There are lots of differences in the way people use vowels, as you move around the country.

What about the second question? What's the difference between consonants and vowels? You might be able to guess one of the differences just by looking at the two lists of words I've just given you. Write some of the first list down on a piece of paper, then underline the consonants. What do you notice? The consonants are found at the beginnings and ends of words. The vowels are in the middle. Even in longer words, it's like this. If you split up the word *postman* into bits (you can find out more about these bits in the entry on **syllable**), you get *post* and *man*. Try *blackbird* and *sadness*. There you are again. Consonants at the beginning and end, vowels in the middle. Of course, you must be prepared for words which look a bit more complicated. Some words don't have a consonant at the end, some don't have one at the beginning, and some (such as *a* and *I*) don't have any consonants in them at all!

There's another important difference between consonants and vowels, which is less obvious. They're made differently. Say some of the consonants – as in *boo, so, fish, me,* and *too*. Can you sense how they're made? For *b* the lips come tightly together. For *t* the tongue hits the roof of the mouth, just behind the teeth. Try it and see. For *f* the bottom lip comes very close to the top teeth, so you get a friction sound. And for *s* and *sh* the tongue comes close to the roof of the mouth, again giving you a friction sound. All the sounds which shut tight or cause a friction sound are consonants. Vowels don't do either of these things. Say *I, oo, ah, oh, ee*. Do you notice how open the mouth is? The tongue is moving up and down, backwards and forwards, but it never closes off the mouth completely, and you never get any friction noise. Go through the word lists I've given you, and check that these guidelines work. Then give yourself a medal for finishing one of the longest entries in this book.

GOVERNMENT SOUND WARNING! Don't mix up sounds and spellings, when you're investigating consonants and vowels. The rule that consonants go at the beginning and end only works for speech. In writing, the spelling rules often put vowels at the end, as in *game* and *like*. If you write the words in phonetic spelling, you'll avoid this problem. Take a look at the entry on **phonetic alphabet**, to see how to do this, then go through the list of symbols at the beginning of this book.

articulation; phonetic alphabet; phonetics; phonology; syllable

context

TEACHER: What's 6 × 7, Blogling?

BLOGLING: Not fair. I've just been in an entry. I'm in 'conditional clause'. Pick on someone else.

TEACHER: I don't care about that, Blogling. What's 6 × 7?

BLOGLING: 40?

TEACHER: I thought as much. You don't know your tables, Blogling.

BLOGLING: Yes, I do, they've got four legs and they're made of wood.

I know, pathetic. But I've just spent 10 minutes trying to think up a better example of how a word can change its meaning from one context to another, and I haven't got anywhere. You have a go. All you have to do is find a word or passage that's unclear or ambiguous, then throw some light on its meaning by 'putting it in context'. *Table* has one meaning when you think about it in the context of numbers. It has another meaning when it's in the context of furniture. You study the **context** of a word when you look at the language surrounding it – or the pictures, of course, if there are any. So, if you saw this headline in the paper:

CALL FOR LONGER SENTENCES

you'd need to look at the context to work out whether it was about evildoers or grammarians. You have to be the judge.

 ambiguous

contour

A **contour** is an outline or shape. The shape goes up and down, or in and out. Hills have contours. People have contours (especially models in Miss World and Mr Hunk competitions). And speech has contours, too. In the case of speech, what goes up and down is the melody of the voice (see **intonation** for more on this). For instance, imagine someone saying this next sentence, in a tone of voice which means 'I can't believe you'd be so stupid!'

Where did you say you put the biscuit tin?

Let's draw the melody underneath. The bottom line is as low as your voice can go, and the top line is as high as it can go. I'll put a dot to stand for each word:

Where did you say you put the biscuit tin?

_____

.   .   .   .

_____

You can see the contour clearly – a gradually rising one. By contrast, here's a gradually falling contour. You'd see this on a 'matter of fact' sentence such as:

Mary had bacon and eggs for breakfast this morning.

There are many other kinds of contours too.

Everyone with normal hearing can recognise these contours, and you use them in your speech all the time. They add a lot of the distinctive meaning to speech. It's interesting to listen to a tape recording, and try to draw the contours of the voice as it moves up and down. If you try it, you'll find that some people have very flat voices, and some are very bouncy. Which are you?

intonation

copula (**kop**-yoo-luh) [ˈkɒpjʊlə]

This is one of the funniest-looking and strangest-sounding words you're ever likely to meet in doing language study. It's from a Latin word which means 'linking' or 'joining', and it describes one of the ways in which we use the forms of the verb *to be* – *am, are, is,* and so on. We often use these forms just to join together two parts of a sentence – like this:

My uncle is a traffic warden.
The children are asleep.

You could almost replace the verb by an 'equals' sign:

My uncle = Traffic warden.
The children = Asleep.

Or even leave it out altogether:

My uncle? Traffic warden.
The children? Asleep.

This is what Tarzan did, you may remember:

Me Tarzan. You Jane.

Though, of course, after reading my book,

Rediscover Grammar, he would have used the copula and said:

I am Tarzan. You are Jane.

So, to sum up, the **copula** is a form of the verb *to be* when it's the *only* verb in the clause.

GOVERNMENT WORD WARNING!
Don't mix up verbs like *is* when they're being used as copulas and when they're being used as 'helping' or 'auxiliary' verbs. There's a big difference between *Mick is a singer* and *Mick is singing*. In the first case, *is* is the copula (*Mick = singer*). In the second case, it's adding to the meaning of the 'main' verb, *singing*. Always check to see if there's a main verb alongside. If there is, you haven't got a copula. When these forms are used as auxiliary verbs, their job isn't to make a link, but to help express the meaning of duration (see the entry on **aspect** for more about this).

auxiliary verb; clause; complement; verb

aspect

corpus (**kaw**-puhs) [ˈkɔːpəs]
plural **corpora** (**kaw**-puh-ruh) [ˈkɔːpərə]

It's happened. 'Tis a miracle. You've been persuaded. Grammar is fun. You can't wait to study how people use it. So what will you do (apart from telling everyone you're not insane)? One thing is to make a collection of what people say or write, and analyse what they do. It could be a collection of newspaper headlines, advertisements, news broadcasts, prayers, everyday conversation – anything! When you make a collection of language data in this way, it's called a **corpus**. *Corpus* is a Latin word, meaning 'body' (yes, it's related in meaning to *corpse*). When linguists study language, they often compile a huge corpus – often, over a million words.

When you've got a corpus, you can find out some interesting things. A few years ago, I collected a small corpus of radio football commentaries. One of the things I wanted to know was which verbs were used most often. I expected *kick* to be the commonest one – well, it is football, after all. In fact, *kick* turned out to be hardly ever used. When commentators are describing a game, they have the players lift, shoot, shaft, drive, thump, blast, and do all sorts of other things to footballs, but nothing as boring as 'kick'. I'd never have guessed that, without my corpus.

 text

count noun and non-count noun

What's the difference between *music* and *a vacuum-cleaner*? Tricky question? Here's a clue. I'm thinking about the words (they're both nouns), not the things they refer to. So, start playing about with their grammar, and see what happens.

- Can you put the word *a* before both of them? No. You can have it before *vacuum-cleaner*, but not before music: you can't say **a music*. (The asterisk is there, remember, to remind you that the following construction is not an acceptable English usage.)
- Can you turn both words into the plural? Can you say *vacuum-cleaners*? Yes. **Musics*? Definitely not.
- Can you use the words without having any article at all? Can you say *I like music*? Of course. What about *I like vacuum-cleaner*? No – you'd sound like a Martian who's not very good at English.
- Can you use the word *some* in front of them? *I want to hear some music*? No problem. *I'd like to use some vacuum-cleaner*? No way.

I could go on, but you've probably got the point. *Vacuum-cleaner* and *music* are different types of noun. There are thousands of nouns like *vacuum-cleaner*: they all take *a*, have plurals, can't be used on their own, and can't go with *some*. Test out *box, telephone*, and *book*, for instance. Likewise, there are thousands of nouns like *music*, which do the opposite: they can't take *a*, they don't have plurals, they can be used on their own, and they can go with *some*. Test *information*, *happiness*, and *mud*, for instance. Grammarians usually call nouns like *vacuum-cleaner* **count** or **countable nouns**. They call nouns like *music* **non-count nouns**, **uncountable nouns**, or **mass nouns**.

GOVERNMENT WORD WARNING! The names suggest that you can count the first group of nouns and that you can't count the second group. This seems to make sense. You can say *one book, two books, three books*, and so on, and you can't say **one music, two musics, three musics*. But actually, it's a more complex matter than the names suggest. In particular, some nouns can be used *either* in a count or a non-count way, depending on what you mean. Take *coffee*, for example. *Coffee tastes wonderful*, someone might say – and, going into a shop, *I'd like some coffee, please*. So far, so good. Just like *music*. But later in the day, going into a snack bar, you might just as easily say, *Two coffees, please* or *I'd like a coffee*! Just like *vacuum-cleaner*. There are lots of nouns that lead a double life, when we want them to. For instance, would you like *some cake for tea*? Or *two teas and a cake*?

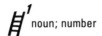 noun; number

creole (**kree**-ohl) [ˈkriːəʊl]

To understand what a creole is, you need to have grasped what a pidgin is first. (Do you know what a **pidgin** is, therefore? If yes, read on. If no, you'd better read that entry now, otherwise the next sentence won't mean a dicky-bird.) A **creole** language emerges when people start using a pidgin language as a mother-tongue. This can easily happen. People start using the pidgin in their homes. They have children, and these grow up using the pidgin as their first language. It then becomes used in all the different ways that you'd use *any* language. What happens to the pidgin, as a result? It expands. It picks up a lot more vocabulary. Its grammar gets more complex. New speech styles emerge. It becomes, in short, as fully developed as any other language.

This process has happened hundreds of times in history. You'll find creole forms of English all over the world, but especially in West Africa, the Caribbean, and several parts of the Pacific. What do they sound like? Here are a few sentences recorded by different creole speakers. The first is written out in standard English; the others are in a special spelling.

When he come out the room he crying he say he fall   (Bahamas)
Mi no mi no yu a go taak   (St Kitts)
('I didn't know you were going to talk')
Dis smol swain i bin go fo maket)   (Cameroon)
('This little piggy went to market')

 pidgin

dactyl see **foot**

declarative (duh-**kla**-ruh-tiv) [dəˈklarətɪv]

The cat *spat* on the mat.
Number 6 *is* the house that Jacques built.
The third example in this entry *is* boring.

If you analyse these sentences, you'll find that each one contains a subject, and this subject goes before any verb. I've made the verbs stand out, so that you can see the point. Sentences with this kind of structure are called **declarative** sentences. Why? If you examine some uses of the word *declare*, I'm sure you'll be able to guess.

'That's codswollop,' Simon declared.
Glamorgan declared at 998 for 3.
Well, I declare!
Lilliput and Trogloditia have just declared war.

After you stare at the word *declare* for more than half a minute, it begins to look ridiculous! But its meaning should be clear enough. *Simon declared?* He said it in an emphatic way. *Glamorgan declared?* They announced that they would bat no more in that innings. *Well, I declare?* I am expressing great astonishment. *The countries have declared war?* They have made a formal announcement that war is to begin. Is there a common thread running through these meanings? *Declare* means to state or make known. And that's the commonest function of a declarative sentence: it expresses a statement. However, you can also use the declarative structure to ask a question – as I've done, several times, at the beginning of this paragraph.

Declaratives are the commonest type of sentence. Almost all the sentences in this entry, so far, are declaratives. (But there are four exceptions. Can you find them? Search hard. I'll give you a clue. Two of them are in these brackets.)

 subject; verb   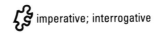 imperative; interrogative

demonstrative (duh-**mon**-struh-tiv) [dəˈmɒnstrətɪv]

Look at this. And that. These are nice. So are those.

What on earth am I talking about? *I* know, because I can see the objects. I'm looking at them now. *You*'ve no idea, until you see them too – or I tell you. Well, I can't expect you to travel all the way to Holyhead, just to see what I'm looking at; and anyway, I'm not looking at anything very interesting, so I might as well tell you:

Look at my pen. And that pencil. These apples are nice. So are those bananas.

The words *this, that, these,* and *those* are obviously pronouns, because they stand in place of the noun phrases *my pen, that pencil, these apples,* and *those bananas.* And they're called **demonstrative** pronouns, because their main job is to *demonstrate* where something is, in relation to the speaker. Two of these pronouns express nearness to the speaker, and two express distance from the speaker. Can you work out which is which? Imagine this. You're standing in front of a greengrocer's display of fruit, and you say:

I'll have some of these apples.

Are they near to you or far away from you? Fairly near. Now what about this?

I'll have some of those apples.

This time, the apples are further away from you.

Is this all clear? That's that, then.

 pronoun   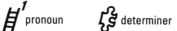 determiner

denotation (dee-noh-**tay**-shuhn) [diːnəʊˈteɪʃn]
and connotation (kon-uh-**tay**-shuhn) [kɒnəˈteɪʃn]

Read this piece of conversation:

MAUDE: What does 'strawberries' mean to you?
CLAUDE: Wimbledon.

It doesn't, of course. A strawberry is a juicy red fruit which . . . But why am I telling you this? You already *know* what a strawberry is. If you don't, you'll have to leave your padded cell, go to the library, and look it up in a dictionary. That's where you'll find the meaning which everyone agrees on – the **denotation** of the word *strawberry*. A dictionary is an enormous list of denotations, in alphabetical order. But the meaning you see in the dictionary isn't the whole story.

If you know about Wimbledon, you can see why Claude gave his answer. Each summer, during the Tennis Championships, they serve strawberries and cream, and this has become a famous part of the event. Eating strawberries at Wimbledon is something Claude does every year, so naturally, when somebody mentions the one idea, he brings to mind the other. *Wimbledon* is a personal meaning for him – though in fact quite a lot of people would have the same feelings, or associations, about strawberries. These personal associations that come with a word are called **connotations**. You don't usually get connotations listed in dictionaries. People may have very different connotations for a word. For some people, the word *smoking* has the connotation of friends and relaxation, for others it has the connotation of hospitals and illness. What does it connote for you?

dental

No. This entry is not about the sounds made by a dentist. It is, though, about teeth. Or rather, it's about what happens when you make a sound by putting the very front of your tongue against your teeth. Sounds made like this are called **dental** consonants. You won't hear them very often, because most English accents don't make much use of dental consonants. The most widely used ones are the *th* sounds of *thin* and *this*, which are made by putting the tip of the tongue *between* the teeth. If you want to be even more precise, you can call these two sounds **interdental**, which means 'between the teeth'. But you'll hear several dental consonants when you listen to the way most Irish people talk. When they pronounce *t* and *d*, for instance, they make these sounds with their tongue against the top teeth. I don't pronounce *my t* and *d* like that: I put my tongue further back, as described in the entry on **alveolar**. Which do you do? Say some words beginning with *t* and try to feel where the front of your tongue is. Against the teeth, or further back? Now make the click sound of *tut tut*. Where does the tongue rest, as you begin to form the sound? For most people, it's against the teeth, this time.

Look after your dentals, and all your other consonants. Read right round the backs of each entry carefully, morning and evening, and come back and see me in six months.

 consonant ⬩ alveolar; labio-dental

determiner

HILARY: I've found a cake.

HILDA: Is this the cake? Whose cake is it?

HILARY: It's not my cake. Is it your cake?

HILDA: Which cake?

HILARY: This cake.

HILDA: That cake's not mine. Look, there's Hiram. Is it his cake?

HILARY: He hasn't had any cake.

HILDA (munching): You have some cake, then.

HILARY: There's not much cake left now!

This mad conversation isn't really about cake, believe it or not. It's about the words that Hilary and Hilda are using immediately in front of the word *cake* in each sentence: *a*, *the*, *my*, *your*, and so on. Have another look at the conversation, and note which ones they are. These words all form a special group in English – a special part of speech, if you like. They all do the same kind of job – telling you which particular noun we're talking about. Is it this one or that one? mine or yours or hers? Words like *some* and *any* tell you about the number or amount of something. They always go in front of a noun, and you can never have two of them together in front of the same noun. You've never heard anyone say **a the cake* or **some this cake*, for instance.

It would be handy to have a single name for all the words which work in this way,

and so linguists have thought one up. They call these words **determiners**, because they 'determine' or 'limit' the noun they go with. The most frequently used determiners are *the* and *a* – the definite and indefinite articles.

GOVERNMENT WORD WARNING! Do you recall seeing words like *this* and *some* before, in another entry? If you do, you're right: they were in the entry on **pronouns** in the Key Stage 3 book. Most of the determiners can be used as pronouns too! How do you tell the difference? Watch.

Some are over there.

What's over there? You don't know. I haven't given you a noun. *Some* stands in for the noun. In other words, it's a pronoun. Now look at this:

Some tapes are over there.

What's over there? Now you know. Tapes. And the word *some* tells you a bit more about them. In other words, it's a determiner.

Don't blame me! That's the way the English language is. If you don't like it, go and speak Chinese, or something.

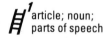 article; noun; parts of speech

 demonstrative; quantifier

deviance (**deev**-yuhns) [ˈdiːviəns]
deviant

YOUNG DALEK: *Grammar English learning I'm.

YOUNG CYBERWOMAN: *I am ingread slot of grammar sbook.

YOUNG MARTIAN: *I n'hatve nlearde to lleps ety.

These three individuals have turned up in an episode of *Star Wars*, and are not getting very far in talking to the other characters. The Dalek is doing quite well, but his word order is wrong. The Cyberwoman has got her words in the right order, but she thinks the word endings go at the beginning. The Martian is in a real muddle: it (there's no difference between male and female on Mars) hasn't yet learned to pronounce words correctly (difficult, anyway, without a mouth), and its spelling is hopeless.

All of these sentences break the rules of the English language, and when a sentence does this we call it **deviant**. Linguists show that a sentence is deviant by putting an asterisk in front of it. Of course, to count as deviant, a sentence doesn't have to be a total mess. Just one tiny errror can make it so. Here are three sentences, each deviant in one small way. Can you spot what it is?

*I should had my tea at six o'clock.
*Look at that red big car.
*Many people examined closely the picture.

By the way, sometimes you find a sentence, and you're not sure whether it's deviant or not. If you ask people whether they think it's normal English, they'll disagree. Try this sentece out on your friends, teachers, parents, or whoever:

The bus Jane got off was very comfortable.

If you're unsure, you can put a question mark in front, like this:

?The bus Jane got off was very comfortable.

You won't often find deviant sentences in written language. Printing errors in spelling are probably the commonest type. (I've left in two such errors in this entry, by the way, to show you what they're like. Did you spot them?) But deviance is quite common in speech, where people have to think on their feet, and sometimes get their grammar muddled up. *In writing, unlikely most is this.

𝄞¹ grammar; usage

diacritic (die-uh-**krit**-ik) [daɪəˈkrɪtɪk]

This is a complicated word for a small thing. The smallest, in fact. Look at these letters, and you'll guess what I'm talking about:

ü, ö, é, à, è, ê, ä, û, î, ù, ẽ, õ, ç, ṣ, a̠, t̚

You can see that each letter has got a small mark with it – usually above it, but sometimes below it. These marks are called **diacritics**. What are they doing there? If you don't know, you may be able to guess if I tell you that *diacritic* comes from a word meaning 'to separate' in ancient Greek. What's being kept separate? Pronunciations. The job of a diacritic is to show you different ways of pronouncing the same letter. In French, for instance, letter *é* is pronounced differently from *e*. In German, *ü* is pronounced differently from *u*. You probably know the everyday term for the diacritics which go on the top of letters: they're called **accents**. But you can have diacritics underneath letters, too. In French, for instance, there's one showing that the letter *c* is to be pronounced [s]. It's called a cedilla (suh**di**luh), and it looks like this: ç. In phonetic spelling, you can even have diacritics which go through the middle of a letter, to show how it should be pronounced – such as [ɫ].

Diacritic marks aren't used very much in English, but you'll sometimes see them. Here are a few I've collected recently:

Naïve Zoë wore a pink negligé when she ate pâté and a soufflé with her fiancé in a café.

𝄞¹ accents; alphabet

digraph (**die**grahf) [ˈdaɪɡrɑːf]

In books published several years ago, you'll often find words printed like this:

encyclopædia œsophagus amœba mediæval

Notice how the *a* and *e*, and the *o* and *e* are joined together to make single letter shapes. When two letters (or 'graphs') link up like this, we call the result a **digraph** (= 'two-graph'). People don't use digraphs much these days: they look old-fashioned. But you'll find several if you learn to write in phonetic spelling. And some reading schemes for young children use them too. Look at the list of phonetic symbols at the front of this book, and you'll see some modern digraphs.

 grapheme; phonetic alphabet

diphthong (**dip**-thong) [ˈdɪpθɒŋ]

Here's a thought for the next time you knock your elbow or bang your thumb, and you say 'Owww!' You've just produced a diphthong. It'll help to take the pain away – unless, of course, you bite your tongue trying to say 'diphthong'. (By the way, learn that spelling by heart: note the *ph* in the middle. *Dipthong* is WRONG!) If you're near a mirror, look at it while you say *ow* as slowly as you can. Or watch while a friend says it – if you can avoid giggling for long enough. (At least mirrors don't giggle!) You'll notice that your mouth starts off quite wide open, and then it closes, and the lips take on a round shape. It's almost as if you start with one vowel – an 'ah' vowel – and end up with another – an 'oo' vowel. And that's really what a **diphthong** is: it's a type of vowel which changes its sound half way through. You'll hear some others in the words *say*, *oh*, *my*, and *ear*. And there's a complete list of all the diphthongs in English in the pronunciation guide at the front of the book.

 consonant and vowel

43

discourse

We
don't
speak
or
write
in
single
words.

Nor do we speak or write in single sentences.
Like this.
With each sentence separated by a pause.
Or on separate lines.
Except in poetry.

What we do is something much more complex – and we do it without even thinking about it. We string our sentences together to make a continuous piece of speech or writing – in other words, a **discourse**.

It's interesting to study the way people build up a discourse. In the spoken language, listen to the way a sports commentary works: you'll hear it 'swinging' between describing the action of the game and talking about what's happened. Or see if you can identify the 'paragraphs' of speech in a radio news bulletin. In the written language, you can look at the way the information on the back of a record sleeve is organised, or how well the instructions for a computer game are written. When you get an English essay or project back, many of the teacher's comments will be to do with the way you've organised your discourse (or failed to!).

I cannot find the beginning of this essay, Brown!
You are supposed to put the conclusion of the project at the end, Smith, not in the middle!

You can get your own back, if you like, and analyse the discourse of your school textbooks, to see if you can do a better job. Start with this one. How do I write these entries? How do I usually make them start? Can you see a pattern in the way I introduce the technical term within the entry? And how do I finish off each entry? Do most entries end quietly, or is there some kind of punch-line? Why don't I stop asking questions, and get on with the next entry?

 conversation; dialogue   text

44

e

echo utterance

ME: This entry is about echo utterances.
YOU: This entry is about *what*?
ME: About echo utterances.
YOU: But I don't know what an echo utterance is.
ME: Yes, you do. You've just used one. And you're about to use another one.
YOU: About to use another one? Never.
ME: You just did.

Are you getting the point? Often, in speech, we take what someone's just said, and give it back to them, changing it just a little. We call the repeated version an **echo utterance** or **echo sentence**. The echo is usually in the form of a question or an exclamation, and it expresses quite a strong feeling. Look at the first example in my little dialogue: you're very surprised, or horrified, or puzzled. But be careful. You can sound very abrupt or rude, if you echo someone's statement:

ME: I'd love another cup of tea.
YOU: You'd love another cup of tea.

Depending on the tone of voice you've used, that *could* mean: 'I wish you'd go. You've been here ages.' Or, of course, it could mean: 'Oh dear. I've just run out of tea!' The danger signals are even stronger if you repeat the sentence *exactly*, and put on the speaker's tone of voice as well:

ME: I'd love another cup of tea.
YOU: Oo, I'd love another cup of tea, would I!

Lastly, it's very unusual to echo yourself. People only do so if they want to draw special attention to what they're saying. People only do so if they want to draw special attention to what they're saying.

question; sentence; statement

-*ed* form see **participle**

elision (uh-**li**-zhn) [əˈlɪʒn]
elide (uh-**lied**) [əˈlaɪd]

Have you ever read any of the 'Just William' stories by Richmal

Crompton? Here's William beginning a political speech in front of his gang:

Ladies an' Gent'men, we're goin' to have a gen'ral election jus' the same as what grown-ups have.

The apostrophes mark sounds which have been left out, and show that William is speaking in a very informal way. When we leave out sounds like this, it's called **elision**. The sounds have been **elided**. Now, here's a question. How do you know which sounds have been omitted? What you have to do is think of the way the words are pronounced when spoken slowly and carefully. The careful pronunciation will give you the 'full' form of the words. You can then work out which sounds are elided in a faster, more casual way of talking. I'm writing this just after breakfast, so let's take the case of bacon and eggs. *And* usually has three sounds: [a], [n], and [d]. But say it more quickly: *bacon'nd eggs*. The *a* has been elided. Say it quicker still. *Bacon 'n' eggs*. That's the *d* elided too. Now it's your turn. Which sounds have been elided in William's sentence at the beginning of this entry?

GOVERNMENT WORD WARNING (if you haven't already read it in the next entry)! Don't mix up **elision** and **ellipsis**. It's **elision** when you leave out sounds inside words. It's **ellipsis** when you leave out words inside sentences.

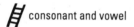 consonant and vowel   ellipsis

ellipsis (uh-**lip**-sis) [ə'lɪpsɪs]
plural **ellipses** (uh-**lip**-seez) [ə'lɪpsiːz]
elliptical (uh-**lip**-ti-kuhl) [ə'lɪptɪkəl]

GAVIN: Where you going?
GARFIELD: Town.
GAVIN: Got a lift?
GARFIELD: Don't think so.

This sounds to you (I hope) like a fairly normal everyday conversation. What makes it normal is that parts of the sentences have been left out. This doesn't cause any problems of understanding, though, does it? You simply 'read in' the missing bits, using your own knowledge of English to work out what's not there. In full, the dialogue would read like this:

Where are you going?
I am going to town.
Have you got a lift?
I don't think so.

When words are left out of sentences in this way, we talk about **ellipsis**. The sentences, you can say, are **elliptical**. Notice how some sentences omit just one word (*are* or *I*), and some omit more than one (*have you* and *I am going to*). When the sentences get very long, many words can be omitted:

GAVIN: Did you go to see the new James Bond film at the Empire last night?
GARFIELD: I did.

Anyone who tells you 'You should always speak in full sentences' is talking through their bonnet. No one would ever answer that question by saying:

I did go to see the new James Bond film at the Empire last night

– not unless they were trying to be funny!

GOVERNMENT WORD WARNING (if you haven't already read it in the previous entry)! Don't mix up **ellipsis** and **elision**. Use **ellipsis** when you talk about words left out of sentences. Use **elision** when you talk about sounds left out of words.

 sentence   elision

emotive meaning (i-**moh**-tiv) [i'məʊtɪv]

In a city street, somewhere in the world, a car pulls up alongside two men in uniform, and gunfire rings out. The car drives away at speed, leaving the men in uniform dead on the ground. Now let's eavesdrop on two conversations about the event. Here's the first:

Our brave freedom fighters have claimed responsibility for the execution of two cowardly traitors.

And here's the second:

Those cowardly terrorists have admitted responsibility for the murder of our two brave patriots.

You can tell, can't you, just from the words used, that the first speaker is on the side of the assassins, and the second speaker is on the other side. Words like *terrorist* and *patriot*, *brave* and *cowardly*, *claim* and *admit*, *murder* and *freedom* are emotional words. They show a person's feelings, and they can arouse deep feelings in those who listen to them. Words which arouse feelings are said to have **emotive meaning**. The emotions can be anything – jealousy, pride, fear, anger, shock, delight – and can vary in strength. In speech, your tone of voice is an important way of signalling the emotions you feel.

It can be difficult to write without using emotive words. Imagine you're the person who writes the BBC news bulletins, and you have to report the above incident in a neutral, unemotional way. What would you write?

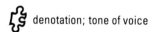 denotation; tone of voice

epigram (**e**-pi-gram) ['epɪgram] or epigraph

Someone once wrote this dedication on the opening page of their essay:

To my English teacher,
without whom
I could be having a great time on the beach right now.

No marks for tact, but full marks for epigram-writing. An **epigram** is often a short piece of verse, which makes a punchy point – or it could be any succinct sentence which says something witty or profound, often with a neat twist of meaning at the end. Here are a couple of famous epigrams, one in verse and one in prose.

Words are like leaves; and where they most abound,
Much fruit of sense beneath is rarely found.   (Pope)
Experience is the name every one gives to their mistakes.
  (Oscar Wilde)

But epigrams aren't found only in poems, novels, and essays. They're often presented as separate pieces of writing. You'll find them in Christmas crackers, in the form of a motto, giving you advice about how to live. You'll find them inscribed on statues and tombstones, summing up the qualities of a person. You'll find them at the beginning of a book or a chapter, giving you a hint of what the text is going to be about. When an epigram is used in this way, it's called an **epigraph**. Historians study the epigraphs of the past, inscribed on ancient walls, coins, and monuments. Modern epigraphs are all around us. In many parts of the country, in fact, you can't walk down the street without seeing them everywhere. They're called – graffiti. Grammar rules, OK?

 aphorism

epithet (**e**-pi-thet) [ˈepiθet]

Listen to bighead Smith talking!
I saw you out with gorgeous Gloria.
I'll meet you near the haunted house.

Which Smith? The bigheaded one. Which Gloria? The gorgeous one. Which house? The haunted one. In each case, we have a word which the speaker is using to sum up the person or thing. A word or phrase which names an important characteristic of a person or thing is called an **epithet**. Epithets are usually adjectives, or nouns used like adjectives. You'll find them not only in everyday speech, but in advertising, newspaper headlines, poetry, and many other contexts. An ad might say:

New Bloxo is gentle.

A news report about Mrs Thatcher, when she was Prime Minister, was headed:

Will the iron lady bend?

The three witches in *Macbeth* are described in the play as:

The weird sisters.

... And they call you Bighead Smith?

Often, nicknames are used in this way. Everyone knows William I by the epithet *The Conqueror*. Richard I was known as *The Lionheart*. A card player might be called *Diamonds*. A teacher called White is bound to end up being called *Chalky*. A girl or boy with glasses might be called *goggles* or *four-eyes*. Do a nickname survey in your school, and see how inventive the epithets are.

GOVERNMENT WORD WARNING! In recent years, the word **epithet** has taken on an extra meaning. You'll hear people say things like: *She shouted all kinds of colourful epithets after him*. In such a context, the word means 'insult' or 'abuse', including the use of swear words.

 adjective; noun

euphony (**yoo**-fuh-nee) [ˈjuːfəni]
euphonious (yoo-**fohn**-yuhs) [juːˈfəʊnɪəs]

Sometimes, when you hear a spoken sentence, you're not impressed. The sounds jangle and clash, and the overall effect is one of harshness. At other times, a sentence might sound so smooth and pleasant that it makes you feel good. You hear the vowels and consonants running together in a gentle, even way, and you take pleasure from the way everything sounds. This effect is called **euphony**, and speech which succeeds in this way is said to be **euphonious**. Of course, in everyday speech, people don't try to be euphonious, and if they did it wouldn't be worth the effort, because people don't have the time to sit back and savour the sounds as they hear them. If someone stopped you in the middle of a conversation and complimented you on your lovely vowels, you'd think they'd escaped. But when you listen to speech which has been carefully constructed, such as in a prayer or a poem, then you expect to hear something beautiful and impressive. Here are two examples of language which sounds euphonious when it is read aloud:

Forlorn! The very word is like a bell
To toll me back from thee to my sole self (Keats)

And lo, the angel of the Lord came upon them, and the glory of the Lord shone round about them (Bible, Luke 2:9)

Unfortunately, there's a catch: people find it difficult to agree about whether sounds, words, voices, or accents are euphonious. Is *envelope* a pleasant-sounding word? or *Birmingham*? or *Jennifer*? Often, when someone says 'Such-and-such is a very euphonious word', all that's meant is 'I like it'!

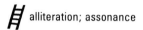 alliteration; assonance

existential sentence (eg-zis-**ten**-shl) [egzɪs'tenʃl]

There's a magic circle on our lawn.
There's a hole in my bucket.
There's a horrible-looking word at the beginning of this entry.

Here's a real test. Who can say what all these sentences have in common? Everyone is correct. They all begin with *There's a*. Now get someone to say them aloud, and listen to how the *there's a* is pronounced. It's said very quickly, without any special emphasis. Sometimes it's said so quickly, in fact, that the first word is dropped altogether, and it comes out like this:

's a magic circle in our garden.

Of course, you could begin with a plural form of the verb, if a plural noun follows:

There are two magic circles in Jane's garden.

And there are a few other verbs you could use, too:

There *exists* an even bigger magic circle in Ferdinand's garden. There came into his mind the thought that any fairies who kept going round in circles must be blind drunk.

Sentences of this kind are called **existential sentences**.

?

Because they are, that's why!

??

Well, because that's the kind of meaning they express. You can take each sentence and 'translate' it like this:

A magic circle exists in our garden.
A hole exists in my bucket.

And so on. Anyway, it's useful to have a term for this kind of sentence. They're actually very common, both in speech and in writing. There are lots of examples in this book, if you go looking. And if nothing else, it's a good conversation-stopper at parties:

OBNOXIOUS GUEST: There's not enough salt in my soup.
YOU: What an interesting existential sentence!

GOVERNMENT WORD WARNING! Notice how different this use of the word *there* is from the same word when it's referring to a particular direction. You can hear both these usages in this next sentence:

There's a red BMW over there.

 sentence

expansion

TWO-YEAR-OLD: Ball.
MUMMY: You've got a ball?
TWO-YEAR-OLD: Kick ball.
MUMMY: Oh, you've kicked the ball, have you? Good girl!
TWO-YEAR-OLD: Ball, um, window.
MUMMY: So you've kicked the ball – where?!!

This child is doing a good job getting the gist of her message across. Being only two, of course, her sentences aren't very well formed yet, and lots of bits are left out. But can you see what her mother is doing? She's checking out what the child is saying by repeating the sentences back in a fuller form. This technique is called **expansion**, and it's especially common between parents and children at around this age, especially when there are other people listening to what's going on. It's a kind of teaching technique, really. And most parents are totally unaware they do it.

Parents of young children aren't the only ones to use expansion, though. Listen to how often your teachers use it, especially when you're not being very forthcoming in your replies!

TEACHER: What were they called, Smith?
SMITH: Arrows, sir.
TEACHER: They were flint-tipped arrows, Smith!

I'm sure you'll hear a conversation like that in the next day or so. Or even the next minute or so, if you don't remember what this entry is all about.

 baby talk; telegrammatic speech holophrase

expletive (eks-**plee**-tiv) [eksˈpliːtɪv]

Strewth! Jeepers! Sugar! ----! ----!

In the last two cases, the expletives, as they say, have been deleted. Well, you have to be careful, when you write a book on language. All sorts of people might read it, and I wouldn't want to give a bad example to innocent minds – you know, young children, parents, teachers . . . So I'll just illustrate the milder ones. An **expletive** is a meaningless word or phrase which you use when you want to let off some emotional steam. It's a kind of exclamation, but with extra force because the words are rude (about sex or bodily functions) or profane (about God or religion). As this is a polite book, I've begun my entry with some fairly mild expletives – mild because people have deliberately softened the original words. *Strewth* is short for *God's truth*. *Jeepers* comes from *Jesus*. *Sugar* starts with the same sound as – well, you know. I'll leave you to think up the other expletives yourself. I'm off to write **eye rhyme**, before I get into trouble.

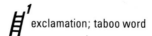 exclamation; taboo word

eye rhyme

Come live with me and be my love,
And we will all the pleasures prove . . .

I hasten to add that this is a linguistic example, not a protestation of passion. It's not me talking, anyway, but the Elizabethan poet, Christopher Marlowe. The lines illustrate an **eye rhyme** – a pair of words which *look* as if they rhyme, but when you say them aloud, they don't. English is full of possible eye rhymes, because many words have changed their pronunciation over the centuries. In Shakespeare's day, *wind* (air movement) used to rhyme with *find*, for instance. It doesn't any more – all we have left is an eye rhyme. Some poets and poetry critics don't like eye rhymes, because they argue that poetry is first and foremost to be spoken, and not read in silence. An eye rhyme, they say, is a cheat. But you'll find quite a number of examples throughout English poetry. Even though the rhyme isn't perfect, there are still some repeated sounds (the [v] sounds of *love* and *prove*, for instance, or the [nd] sounds of *wind* and *find*), and the poet can make use of these in constructing the network of sound effects that help to convey the poem's meaning. There are limits, though. I don't think any poet would make an eye rhyme out of *through* and *cough*, for instance.

 rhyme

finite (**fie**-niet) ['faɪnaɪt] and nonfinite

I am going to ask you some questions which you won't be able to answer – but read this fragment of a sentence first:

Laughing happily . . .

Who's laughing happily? One person or more than one? And when does the laughing take place? Now? In the future? In the past? The correct answer is 'don't know' to all these questions.

'Not fair', you might be thinking. Give us some more of the sentence and we'd be able to answer them. Fair point, but hold on a moment while I give you some questions you *can* answer – after you've read this fragment:

. . . was happy.

Now who's happy? One person or more than one? And when does the happiness take place? Now? In the future? In the past?

First answer: One person. How do you know? Because the fragment is '*was* happy'. If it had been more than one, it would have been '*were* happy'. Second answer: In the past. How do you know? Because it said *was*, and not *is* or *will be*.

56

What's this all about? (I thought you'd never ask.) You can tell from these examples that forms of the verb give you two different kinds of information. Some forms (such as *was*) tell you about the time of the action and the number of people involved; some forms (such as *laughing*) tell you none of this. Linguists call the forms like *was* the **finite** forms of the verb, and the others the **nonfinite** forms. Why? (I wish I'd never started this entry.) Well, what does 'finite' usually mean? It means you've got a limited number of something. If you've got a finite number of eggs, you can count them. *Was* is limited in a similar way. It's tied down to one particular use – past time, and a single person. It's finite in its use. *Laughing*, however, isn't restricted at all. It's not limited to past time – or to any time. You can use it anywhere – like this:

Laughing happily, Judy walked down the street. (past)
I can see Judy, laughing happily. (present)
Next week Judy will arrive home, laughing happily. (future)

Here are some other finite forms:

Judy *is* happy (present time, one person involved)
Judy *looks* well (present time, one person involved, third person only)
John *looked* well (past time)
I *am* (present time, one person involved, first person only)

Apart from the form ending in -ing (as in *laughing*), there are two other nonfinite forms:

- the infinitive form, as in *to go, to do*;
- forms like *taken* and *stolen* (see the entry on **participle** for more about these).

Check out that these are indeed nonfinite forms by asking time, person, and number questions.

Taken out to dinner, I/you/they felt/feel/will feel better.
I am/was/will be ready to finish this entry now.

And about time too.

 infinitive; number; person; tense; verb   participle

focus (**foh**-kuhs) [ˈfəʊkəs]

Find someone who's waiting for some excitement to enter their life, and give them the chance to do this experiment. They'll be eternally grateful. All they have to do is read these aloud. All *you* have to do is listen carefully and note which word in each sentence is said most loudly.

SID: Have we got some food left?
DAD: I've got some biscuits.
SID: We haven't got any sandwiches, then?
DAD: I've got a ham sandwich, I think.

Most people will say *food*, in the first sentence, *biscuits* in the second, *sandwiches* in the third, and *ham* in the fourth. There might be some variations, but it's most unlikely that anyone will have made *some* the loudest word in the first sentence, or *I* in the second. Why? People emphasise the word they think is the most important, and this word is called the **focus** of the sentence. The focused word is usually the new bit of information in a sentence. In the first sentence, Sid's mind and stomach are in agreement, so *food* is the focus. Because the focus is on food, Dad makes the word *biscuits* stand out in his sentence. That's the new bit of information. Sid keeps it up, focusing on *sandwiches*. And Dad responds, putting the focus on *ham*, which is the word *he* wants to draw attention to. In speech, it's all done through the use of melody and loudness (see the entry on **intonation**, for more about this). In writing, you have to use underlining or special printing to make a focused word stand out (as I did two sentences ago – see the *he*?). You can focus on almost any word you want, in a sentence – as long as it makes sense to do so. *Almost* any word. Almost *any* word.

 given; intonation; stress

foot

DAWN: What's a foot?
SHAWN: Nothing, as far as I know.

Shawn, can we be serious, here, for a minute? It's *a foot* not *afoot*, as you well know. And before you chip in again, I do *not* mean the odorous object at the end of your leg. I'm talking about poetry – or, at least, certain kinds of poetry. A **foot** is a useful word for talking about the regular units of rhythm which poets often use in constructing lines of verse. How many units of rhythm can you hear in this line? (Tap it out before you answer.)

The curfew tolls the knell of parting day.

There are five 'te-*tum*' units – five feet. Now try this one:

The poplars are felled, farewell to the shade.

Here we have four feet: 'te-*tum* te-te-*tum* te-*tum* te-te-*tum*'.

If you've got the idea, you can now start working out what all the possibilities are: te-*tum*, *tum*-te, te-te-*tum*, *tum*-te-te, and so on. Mind you, you'll find it a bit awkward saying 'tum-te-tum' all the time. Better to use the technical terms that literary scholars have thought up to describe the commonest types of feet.

- A te-*tum* pattern is called an **iamb** (pronounced **ie**-am), or **iambic foot** (ie-**am**-bik).
- A *tum*-te is called a **trochee** (pronounced **troh**-kee), or **trochaic foot** (truh-**kay**-ik).
- Two loud syllables together ('*tum-tum*') is called a **spondee** (pronounced **spond**-dee), or **spondaic foot** (spon-**day**-ik).
- *Tum*-te-te is called a **dactyl** (pronounced **dak**-til), or **dactylic foot** (dak-**til**-ik).
- Te-te-*tum* is called an **anapaest** (pronounced **an**-uh-peest), or **anapaestic foot** (an-uh-**pees**-tik).

If you've taken in that lot, you deserve a cuppa. And after writing it, so do I. We carry on in five minutes.

Te tum or not te tum....

Right. Better? Now, why have I told you about types of feet? Well, when you listen to lines of poetry, it's interesting to be able to talk about how the poet changes the rhythm to convey different kinds of effect. The technical terms can help you sum up what's happening in a line. If you feel the pace of the poem changing, or the mood changing, it may well be because the poet has changed the rhythm (or **metre**, as rhythm is often called in poetry).

But beware! Don't go off with the idea that every line of poetry has to be made up of a regular series of feet. Most modern poetry doesn't work like that. The units of rhythm are more varied and less predictable, and you have to think of the way the 'weight' of the line alters, as you move from one part to the next. Read these lines from T S Eliot aloud, and you'll hear what I mean.

And under the oppression of the silent fog
The tolling bell
Measures time not our time, rung by the unhurried
Ground swell, a time older than the time of chronometers . . .

Can you hear how the short line slows you down, and starts off in your mind the sound of the bell, which is then taken up in the next lines with the slow repetition of the word *time*? Try reading it so that *time* really stands out. I think it's brilliantly done. Do you?

 metre; rhythm   stress

foregrounded (**faw**-grown-did) [ˈfɔːɡraʊndɪd]
foregrounding

Where do you usually talk about 'foreground' and 'background'? Yes, paintings and photographs. If something is in the foreground, it stands out. Well, you can use the same terms for talking about language, too, with more or less the same meaning. You bring a bit of language into the foreground when you make it stand out from its surroundings. When you do that, you can say that the item of language has been **foregrounded**. Here are three examples of foregrounding. You shouldn't have any difficulty in spotting what they are.

My mum makes marshmallows on Mondays.
Are you going to the Olde Tyme dance tonight?
Send us, O Lord, your forgiveness.

Wasn't it the truth? An abnormal number of [m] sounds, in the first sentence (see the entry on **alliteration**, for more about this). An old-fashioned spelling in the second sentence. And the use of the special greeting word *O*, in the third sentence, which these days you find only in religious contexts. Foregrounding is especially important in literature, where authors are always striving to make the language move in fresh directions. But you'll also find it in advertising, prayers, newspapers, and indeed in any setting where people want their language to be distinctive. I usually try for a special effect at the beginning and end of each entry in this book. I like to catch your attention by starting off with a question, a task, a piece of dialogue, or the like – not the kind of thing you'd normally find in an *A to Z*. And I like to finish off with a bang, and not a whimper, by doing something different or unexpected at the end. Like this. No, hang on, that's not very noticeably foregrounded. LIKE THIS.

figure of speech; metre; rhyme   alliteration; assonance

free direct speech and free indirect speech

Hands up who can recall the difference between direct and indirect speech. Yes, Martha?

Martha said, 'I can, because I'm a good girl, and I read *Language A to Z for Key Stage 3*.'

Martha said she could, because she was a good girl, and she had read *Language A to Z* for Key Stage 3.

Well done, Martha! You are a real cree – I mean credit to the class. With direct speech, you can see what's said directly, as if you had it on a tape recorder. The inverted commas show you. So, what's **free direct speech**? Here's an example, in the middle of this short paragraph from my latest murder story.

Hilary crept into the back room. She saw the curtains, dragged together roughly, as if – as if – There's someone behind them. I'm sure there's someone behind them. I must stay calm. She reached for the light.

This is a story set in the past, as you can tell from the verbs *crept* and *saw*, and *I'm* telling the story. But suddenly, in the third and fourth sentence, Hilary starts to tell the story – or, at least, she uses her own words, not mine. It's a kind of direct speech, except that I haven't put *Hilary said*, or used inverted commas. To do so would interfere with the build-up of excitement. Switching from one style to the other can heighten the atmosphere, and add to the drama. When you use direct speech in this way, it's called **free direct speech**.

Now read on:

She paused. That would be stupid. Wouldn't that be exactly what he wanted her to do? She'd be a sitting duck, framed in the doorway. She mustn't be such a fool! She must think! Think!

What's happened this time? We start off, once again, with me telling the story in past time. Then, in the second sentence, I switch styles, and it's as if you were inside Hilary's head. You can hear her thinking. The language is like indirect speech, except that there's no *Hilary thought* at the beginning, and several of the features of direct speech are retained, such as questions and commands. This interesting mixture of the two styles is called **free indirect speech**. Many authors have used it to help represent a character's stream of thought (or 'stream of consciousness', as it's often called).

I know you're curious, so I'll let you into a secret. The murderer is –

Sorry about this. Joan from Longman has just rung up to say I must get on with fricatives, as they want to publish this book before the year 2000. You might get a clue if you read the entry on **parallelism**, though.

 direct speech

fricative (fri-kuh-tiv) ['frɪkətɪv]

You've done science. You know what friction is. And you know that it can make a noise. When something rubs against something else, you can often hear the friction: it's audible. Or when air rushes through a narrow gap, such as wind blowing through the branches of a tree: it's audible. In speech, the air which comes up from the lungs can cause audible friction, too. If you put your lips very close together, as if you were about to blow out a candle, and you blow hard, you'll hear the sound of the friction, as the air passes through the lips. In speech, we use this kind of friction to make several different sounds, called **fricatives**. Listen to the first sounds of *fee* [f], *van* [v], *thin* [θ], *this* [ð], *see* [s], *zoo* [z], *she* [ʃ], and *he* [h], and the sound spelled with an *s* in *fusion* [ʒ]. They're all fricatives.

The fricative consonants of English comprise some of the commonest sounds in the language (e.g. [s]) as well as some of the rarest sounds (e.g. [ʒ], which hardly ever comes at the beginning or end of a word). If you've been studying other languages, you may well have discovered other fricatives. For instance, Spanish uses both lips to make fricatives. Welsh has one towards the back of the mouth, as in *bach* (you can hear it in Scots *loch*, too). Poets in particular love fricatives, as you can stretch the sound out, and make all kinds of interesting effects with them. Here's a lineful of fricatives, from Robert Browning:

Leave the flesh to the fate it was fit for! the
   spirit be thine!

And here's a short sentence full of fricatives, with love and kisses from me, to end this entry. Seventeen in there, in fact. Can you find them all? (I'm ignoring the [r]'s.)

 consonant

front and back

Useful things, mouths. Helpful for eating, whistling, breathing, kissing – and talking. And when you use a mouth for talking, you use all parts of it. Now: stand by for a really obvious pair of terms. If you make sounds at the front of the mouth, they're called **front** sounds. And if you make sounds at the back of your mouth, they're called, wait for it, **back** sounds. Too easy? 'A' grades for everyone? All right. Here's something a bit trickier. You can make vowel sounds with the front part of your tongue (**front vowels**) or with the back part of your tongue (**back vowels**). So can you tell which is which? You really have to concentrate hard, to feel where your tongue is.

Here are three front vowels in English:
   the sound of *ee* in *feet* /iː/
   the sound of *e* in *get* /e/
   the sound of *a* in *hat* /a/

And here are three back vowels:
the sound of *oo* in *loo* /u:/
the sound of *aw* in *saw* /ɔ:/
the sound of *ah* in *ah* /a:/

Here's a useful trick which can help you feel where vowels are made in the mouth. Make a vowel sound, such as the /i:/ of *feet*. Now, don't move your tongue at all, and breathe in sharply. You'll feel the rush of cold air going past the front part of the tongue, towards the top of the mouth, and this tells you the position your tongue is in. Next, do the same with the /a:/ of *ah*. This time the air will reach the very back of your mouth. The trick doesn't work well for all vowels, but it helps for some of them. Try it – but preferably only when you're in class, or on your own. If you walk down the street making vowel noises and breathing in sharply, the men in white coats will soon be paying you a visit.

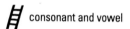 consonant and vowel

generic reference (juh-**ne**-rik) [ʤəˈnerɪk]

The parrot can be a very talkative bird.

Which parrot? Any parrot, of course. I'm not talking about a particular parrot. I'm talking about parrots in general. In fact, I could have said:

Parrots can be very talkative birds.

I can't understand it – Another huge telephone bill!

The parrot here means 'the class of parrots' – *all* parrots. When a noun is used in this way, referring to a whole class of objects, we say it has **generic reference**. Here are some other generic uses of nouns:

Lilliputians are small.
The Lilliputians are small.
The Lilliputian is small.
A Lilliputian is small.

Each of these sentences has a generic meaning: *all* Lilliputians are small. And what's particularly interesting about this kind of example is that, suddenly, there isn't a difference in meaning any more between singular and plural, or between the definite and indefinite article. When a noun is used in a generic way, these differences aren't important any longer. Mind you, it's the only time in English when you get these differences cancelling out. So please don't feel sick as a parrot about it. Or even sick as parrots.

 noun

given and new

PETER: Which video did you watch last night?
PETRA: *The Curse of the Hatchet-Man's Granny.*

That's how you'd normally say it. This kind of answer would be most unusual:

PETRA: Last night I watched the video called *The Curse of the Hatchet-Man's Granny.*

Why? Because there's no point. What's the point in Petra saying all over again what Peter has just said? She can take it for granted. So, what can we call the information in a sentence which you already know about, and the information which is new to you? In a brilliant fit of inspiration, linguists have come up with the terms **given** information for the first and **new** information for the second. Pretty clever, eh?

 discourse: focus

glottis (**glo**-tis) ['glɒtɪs]
glottal (**glo**-tl) ['glɒtl]

Right. Another Mastermind question. Where's your glottis? (No, it's not under your arm, Jopplesthwaite.) It's in your throat. It's the name given to the space between your vocal cords. If you make a speech sound there, it's called a **glottal** sound. [h], as in *hi*, is one such sound. The friction noise that you can hear comes from the air rushing past the vocal cords. Another glottal sound is the one you hear in certain accents of English – especially in the accents influenced by the Cockney speech of London. You'll hear thousands in any episode of *EastEnders*. It's called a **glottal stop**. Listen out for it especially in words like *bottle*, when it replaces the *t*. In the sentence *She's gotta lotta bottle*, you often hear each *t* replaced by a glottal stop. In fact, the use of the glottal stop is one of the fastest spreading sounds at the moment in British English. But not everyone likes them. If your family doesn't use them in its accent, and *you* start using them, you'll soon hear about it. They'll soon be telling you to 'pronounce your *t*'s'.

fricative; plosive; vocal cords

grapheme (**gra**-feem) ['grafiːm]

No prizes for seeing what's going on here:

Correct. They are all (but one) kinds of 'A'. Some are capitals, and some are small letters. Several different kinds of lettering are used (they're called different **typefaces**). But they are definitely all (but one) different kinds of 'A'. I could do the same with B, C, D, and so on up to Z. There are 26 letters in English, and each of them turns up in all kinds of shapes and sizes. Which reminds, me, I haven't shown you sizes yet:

a a **a a**

Look in a newspaper, and you'll see plenty of different sizes. In language study, it's useful to have a term for a basic 'letter' – the 'A-ness' which you can see in all of the A-shapes. That term is **grapheme**. So you can now say: there are 26 graphemes in English. And one more thing. What do we call the different shapes that each grapheme can have? They're **graphs**. (Forget maths. This is linguistics.) Graphemes are often written in angle brackets, like this: <a>. At the top of this entry I've shown you six graphs all representing the same grapheme, <a>. And there was one graph representing the grapheme <w>. If you've got a moment, go graph collecting. See how many different kinds you can find.

 alphabet    digraph; graphology

graphology (gruh-**fol**-uh-jee) [grəˈfɒlədʒi]

You're at your favourite seaside resort, walking along the prom. There are fruit machines, hot dog stalls, video games, and interesting arcades. Then you see a small caravan. It says, 'Madame

Zaza, graphologist'. You go in. What will she do to you? She will try to read your character or your fortune from a sample of your handwriting. For instance, if you cross your *t*'s with a long stroke, Madame Zaza might tell you that you have a strong desire to protect others. If the cross stroke of the *t* is separated from the down stroke – coming after it – she might say that you're a hasty person, not in control of your thoughts. If you have a boyfriend or girlfriend with you, she might compare your two styles of handwriting to see if they're similar – otherwise, you'll never make a happy couple.

Got all that? Good. Now, put it on one side for the moment, because when you come across the word **graphology** in a language discussion, it *doesn't* refer to Madame Zaza's domain. It has a different meaning: the study of the writing system of a language. It's the study of the letters, the spelling rules, the punctuation marks, and any other symbols that are used – in short, everything that happens when you write or print a language. 'The graphology of English is very interesting,' somebody might say. And so it is.

alphabet; punctuation; upper case   grapheme

group genitive (je-nuh-tiv) [ˈdʒenətɪv]

Close your eyes, and think back to the days long long ago when you were at Key Stage 3. Do you remember, when the sun was shining and the birds twittered in the trees, and the waves lapped gently along the sea shore, we talked together about the genitive case? Ah, happy days. And what *was* the genitive case?

I said: What was the genitive case?

YOU: Shame, I was just nodding off. Anyway, you haven't told us to open our eyes yet.
ME: Sorry. Open your eyes.

But come to think of it, if you've got your eyes closed, you can't be reading this, so there's no point in my telling you. Anyway, you don't have to open your eyes to remember that the genitive case is the name you give to a noun when it's got an -'s or -s' ending. Now here's a Key Stage 4 Fact: you can actually have a *phrase* with a genitive ending. Here are some examples:

That's *someone else*'s problem.
You are sitting on *the Queen of Sheba*'s spectacles.
I've got *an hour and a half*'s homework.

This use of the genitive is called the **group genitive**, because the genitive is being added to a group of words. But be careful when you try to use this construction. Into the classroom walks a teacher with a bald head carrying a cat. If you want to describe him, I wouldn't say:

Look at the teacher with the cat's bald head.

For obvious reasons!

目¹ case; noun

haiku (**hie**-koo) [ˈhaɪkuː]

This is a type of poem from Japan which became quite popular among Western poets earlier this century. It's a very simple form. There are only three lines. The first line has five syllables; the second has seven; and the third has five. The whole poem must express a single image or idea. It's a kind of quick snapshot in words. Sounds easy, but actually it's very difficult to do well in English, because

English rhythm is different from Japanese rhythm. I've had a go, anyway, to give you the general idea.

A mountain at dusk.
Flickering lights behind leaves.
Homes or fallen stars?

Your turn?

目 syllable

head

What have these three constructions got in common?

my crazy American cousins
have been snoring
very loudly

You won't get it right unless you've spotted that they're all **phrases**. (What? You've forgotten about phrases? But I spent *hours* writing all those entries in the Key Stage 3 book – noun phrase, verb phrase, adverb phrase, adjective phrase, prepositional phrase. There was even a separate entry on **phrase** itself. Right. That's it. Finish. No more entries. Write your own book.)

(*one phone call later*)

Oh. That was Joan, my publisher from Longman. She says she's extremely sorry, but if I don't carry on with this book she will personally drop a copy of *A Comprehensive Grammar of the English Language* on my big toe. That's no mean threat. That grammar weighs about 2.4 kilos. So, onwards. I described five kinds of phrase in Key Stage 3, but there are only three examples above. Can you work out which two are missing? Start with the three I've given you. What's *my crazy American cousins*? A noun phrase. How do you know? Because the chief word in it is *cousins*, and that's a noun. Now *have been snoring*. That's a verb phrase. How do you know? Because the chief word in it is *snoring*, and that's a verb. And *very loudly*? That's an adverb phrase – because the chief word in it is an adverb, *loudly*. So, what's missing? An adjective phrase, such as *very interesting*, where the chief word is an adjective. And a prepositional phrase, such as *in the garden*, where the word that controls the construction is the preposition *in*.

After all that, I've forgotten to tell you what a **head** is. Well, I was upset. The **head** of a phrase is the chief word in the phrase – the word which controls how the phrase is used in a sentence. Now you know. And I think I'll go and read my entry on **haiku** again, to calm my nerves.

^{1} phrase (but I expect you've got that message now)

historic present

You'll never believe this. Last Christmas, I'm at a party, and I see this drunk trying to strike a match. He's cursing away. 'What's the matter?', I ask. 'Stupid match won't work,' says he. 'Why not?', I ask. 'Dunno,' the drunk replies. 'It was all right when I struck it last time.'

Now, what does this old story prove? The important point is –

FOREIGN LEARNER: Excuse, please?
ME: Pardon?
FOREIGN LEARNER: You use present tense of verb. How you can do that?
ME: Why not?
FOREIGN LEARNER: Because your story, she happen last year. It not happen *now*.

Well spotted, Foreign Learner. But I *did* do it, didn't I? And it didn't sound odd, did it? In fact, it helped to make the story come alive. Compare it with this version:

Last Christmas, I was at a party, and I saw this drunk trying to strike a match. He was cursing away. 'What's the matter?', I asked. 'Stupid match won't work,' said he. 'Why not?', I asked. 'Dunno,' the drunk replied. 'It was all right when I struck it last time.'

That's the interesting thing about the present tense in English. You can use it in all kinds of different ways. If you tell a story from the past using the present tense, it becomes more dramatic and immediate – as if it's happening now. And when you use the present tense in this way, it's called the **historic present**. If you want to collect some good examples, listen to the way comedians tell stories on television. There you are – what more do you want? Official instructions to go and watch TV. And all in the cause of grammar.

 present tense

holophrase (**ho**-luh-frayz) [ˈhɒləfreɪz]

Here's the complete collection of all the things Susie, aged 15 months, said in one day:

there	allgone
mummy	more
teddy	dink (= drink)
no	woof
dindin	poon (= spoon)

Not much, is it! But then, she was asleep about 60 per cent of the time, and guzzling about 20 per cent of the time, so there wasn't much time left for talking. What do you notice, though, about all her sentences? They're all short – just one element long. Most are just one word, and in one case there are two words run together (*allgone*). The meaning of each utterance, though, is 'larger' than that of a single word. Each of these utterances is doing the job of a whole sentence. *Allgone*, for instance, meant 'My food is allgone'. *Teddy* meant 'I want my teddy'. When a single element does the job of a whole sentence, it's called a **holophrase**. Children speak in holophrases when they begin to use their first words, at around 12 months of age, and they carry on like this for about six months or so. Then they start joining words together, and their utterances begin to look like real sentences. So, if you want to study holophrases you have to be quick, otherwise you'll miss them.

baby talk; telegrammatic speech

homographs see homonyms

homonyms (**ho**-muh-nimz) ['homənɪmz]

DINER: Waiter, there's something wrong with my bill.
WAITER: Oh, I'm sorry, sir, I'll get you a hanky.

Boom, boom! That's a homonym joke. **Homonyms** are words which are the same in form but different in meaning. 'Having the same form' means that they sound the same *and* look the same. So, *bill* (in the sense of money) and *bill* (in the sense of beak or nose) are homonyms. So are *bear* (the animal) and *bear* (to carry), and *ear* (of the body) and *ear* (of corn). Many of the awful jokes in joke books and Christmas crackers are based on homonyms.

This next joke is slightly different, though.

DORIS: Have you heard the story about the peacock?
HORACE: No.
DORIS: What a pity. It's such a beautiful tale/tail.

That joke only works in speech. If you write it down, you have to choose one or other of the spellings, and it rather spoils the effect. *Tale* and *tail* sound the same, but they don't look the same. Words of this kind are called **homophones** (meaning 'same sounds'). There are thousands of examples in English: *rode* and *rowed*, *threw* and *through*, *told* and *tolled* . . .

You can also have the opposite effect – words which look the same, but which don't sound the same. These are called **homographs** (meaning 'same letters'). *Wind* (the breeze) and *wind* (a clock) are homographs. So are *tear* (some paper) and *tear* (from your eye). Homograph jokes are for the eye, not the ear. Lead on, as the sharpener said to the pencil.

ambiguous   polysemic

homophones see **homonyms**

hyperbole (hie-**per**-buh-lee) [haɪˈpɜːbəliː]

YOU: That last entry was absolutely fantastic.
ME: Oh, surely not.
YOU: Yes, it was definitely the best entry in the history of the world.
ME: Gosh, really?
YOU: Without a shadow of a doubt. And by the way, could you lend me a pound?

When you go over the top like this, using language, it's called **hyperbole**. Hyperbole is a figure of speech in which you use wild exaggeration to make an effect. Everyday conversation makes use of it all the time. If you've ever said something like *There were thousands of people at the disco* (though the room can only hold 200 at most) or *There are millions of ants in the dining room* (when actually there are 42), you've used hyperbole. It can be a very effective way of dramatically drawing attention to a point. People listen when you exaggerate – as long as you don't do it all the time. Here's a famous example of hyperbole, from Hamlet:

I loved Ophelia: forty thousand brothers
Could not, with all their quantity of love,
Make up my sum.

Personally, I'm not one for using hyperbole, and certainly never in an entry like this – not in a million years.

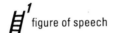 figure of speech   litotes

hypernyms see **hyponyms**

hyponyms (**hie**-puh-nimz) [ˈhaɪpənɪmz]
hyponymy (hie-**pon**-i-mee) [haɪˈpɒnɪmi]

What's a daffodil?   A sort of flower.
What's an elephant?   A sort of animal.
What's scarlet?   A sort of red.
What's a banana?

You can answer that one yourself. Or, at least, you can if you've picked up the pattern: an X is a sort of Y. This is one of the main ways in which words relate to each other in meaning. The relationship is one of *inclusion*: a *daffodil* is included in the class of *flowers*; a *banana* is included in the class of *fruit*; and so on. You can work the other way round, too:

What are flowers?   Daffodils, tulips . . .
What are animals?   Elephants, cats . . .

This kind of relationship between words is called **hyponymy**. The name is based on the more familiar terms of **synonymy** and

antonymy (you'll find more on those in the Key Stage 3 book). Synonymy refers to pairs of words which have the same meaning; antonymy to pairs of words which have opposite meanings; and **hyponymy**, now, for pairs of words where one word is included within the other. *Daffodil* and *tulip*, we say, are hyponyms of *flower*. And what is *flower*? That's the **hypernym** (**hie**-puh-nim) of *daffodil*, *tulip*, and all the other flowers. Remembering the difference between these two terms can be tricky, so think of it like this:

- the *hypernym* is the 'larger', more general word – just as a *hyperstore* is a very large store.
- the *hyponym* is the 'smaller', more specific word – it goes underneath, just as a *hypodermic* needle goes underneath the skin.

But beware! It isn't always easy to find a hypernym for a word. What's a teacher? A kind of —? person? human being? torturer? slave?

GOVERNMENT WORD WARNING! Did you notice that **hyponym** and **hypernym** are pronounced in the same way. The only way to distinguish them in speech is to exaggerate the pronunciation of the second syllable, and say (hie-**per**-nim) and (hie-**poh**-nim). It sounds odd, but it works.

📐¹ antonyms; synonyms

iambic foot see **foot**

ideogram (i-dee-oh-gram) [ˈɪdɪəʊgram]

You are leading an expedition in search of the lost city of Phon. After a long journey, you stumble across the ruins of an old building. On the wall are some carved symbols. You study them carefully. The first symbol looks like a sun: there's a circle with rays coming out from it. The second looks like an ornate chair – a throne, perhaps. The third looks like a knife. The fourth looks like a pin man, but the body is in half. You try to interpret the symbols: perhaps this is the place where people (pin man) were killed (body in two) with a knife and offered as a sacrifice to the sun god (throne + sun). The carvings look recent. You think maybe you'll go home now.

You may not have found any treasure, but you *have* found some **ideograms** (or **ideographs**) – the pictorial units of an early writing system. The symbols don't represent words or sounds, as modern writing systems do, but stand for objects or ideas directly. Ancient ways of writing often used ideograms. Chinese writing was like this originally, as was the ancient Egyptian system of writing (usually called **hieroglyphics** (hie-ruh-**gli**-fiks)). But Chinese isn't like this now. The writing has changed over the centuries. If you look at Chinese characters, you won't be able to read them in the way our explorers did.

English doesn't have any ideograms in its writing system, but you'll find plenty of examples of ideograms every time you go out. Look at the street sign telling you there are roadworks ahead, or the shop sign telling you that no smoking is allowed. I wonder what future explorers will make of them, if ever our cities get lost?

 alphabet; logogram

idiolect (**i**-dee-oh-lekt) [ˈɪdɪəʊlekt]

No, this is not a dialect spoken by idiots. The prefix *idio-* means 'personal' in Greek – as in the word *idiosyncrasy*, which means a personal habit or eccentricity. And **idiolect** is your own personal dialect. It's the kind of language which you – Jim, Jean, Mary, or whatever your name is – make use of, and which makes you different from everyone else. If you think about it, there are so many ways in which our vowels, consonants, voice qualities, words, and sentence patterns differ from person to person that you'd be very unlikely to find two people who had exactly the same way of using language. Everyone has their own idiolect.

There are many ways to check this out. Do you and your friends have exactly the same feelings about words and sentences? Which words do you like? Which do you hate? Which sound odd? Which are embarrassing? You'll find many differences of opinion. Or do this: choose a couple of pages from an advanced dictionary, and make a list of all the words which are defined there. Everyone has to say which words on the list they often use, which words they occasionally use, which words they never use but do understand, and which words they don't understand at all. I should be very surprised if two people ever came up with the same results.

An idiolect is a bit like having your own linguistic fingerprints, really – except that you can imitate or forge language, but you can't forge fingerprints.

 dialect

imperative (im-**pe**-ruh-tiv) [ɪmˈperətɪv]

FAIRY GODFATHER: It is imperative that you return to the castle before midnight.

BARBARELLA: And if I don't, godfather?

FAIRY GODFATHER: If you don't, we turn you into a pumpkin – the hard way.

Barbarella is in no doubt. She must return, or else. Imperative means 'must'. We usually use verbs when we tell people (or animals) what they must do.

Sit. Stay. Jump. Heel. Come.

(Obviously part of a dialogue with a tame boyfriend.) Notice how much use is made of the verb. When giving commands, a language often puts the verb into a special form, called the **imperative**. It's easy in English, because the chief imperative form is the simplest one – the basic form of the verb, without any endings. So we say *sit* – not *sit-be* or *sittez*, or the like. Utterances which have this kind of verb in them are called **imperative sentences**. Here are some typical cases:

Open the door.
Do come in.
Put the book on the table.
Don't put the book on the table.
Get knotted.

Imperatives don't usually have a subject, except in cases like *You sit down this minute!* or *Nobody move!*, where you're being very insistent.

GOVERNMENT WORD WARNING! People usually think of imperatives as being directed towards the person they're talking to – the second person (*you*). But there are other forms. In particular, you can command *yourself* to do something (and why not?), and have a first person imperative. You signal this by beginning the sentence with *let*. Now, can I think of some good examples of that? Let me see. Yes, let's use these two.

⌗¹ verb   🧩 declarative; interrogative; mood

impersonal style

Beep. Beep. Beep. Beep. Beep. Bee-ee-eep.
This is the six o'clock news. Now, where shall I start this evening? Oh, yes. Listen, I've just heard a splendid report from California that some professor – a nut-case, if you ask me – has thought up a new technique for taking pictures of flying saucers. I haven't grasped all of it yet, but . . .

Not a very likely style, I admit. In real life, after the beeps, it would probably go something like this:

This is the six o'clock news. A report from California states that a university professor has invented a new technique for photographing unidentified flying objects. The technique appears to be based on . . .

When people speak or write in this last style, it's often called **impersonal**. An **impersonal style** is, quite simply, one where you try to distance yourself from what you're saying or writing. People do this on very formal occasions, or when they want to state something objectively, without bias or emotion – when they're reading the news, for instance. Textbooks are often written in an impersonal style, especially when the writer is giving a general account of events:

The mixture is to be poured into a test tube.
It is recommended that only a small drop of nitroglycerine be used.

The passive construction (see the entry on **voice**, for more about this) is very common in this kind of language, as are such phrases as *It appears* and *There seem*, and the use of the pronoun *one* (*If one isn't careful, one could easily fall off one's horse*).

In a **personal style**, you put yourself into the language. The text is spattered with first person pronouns (e.g. *I*, *us*, *myself*), attitude expressions (e.g. *frankly*, *to be fair*), personal impressions (e.g. *charming*, *superb*), and interactive phrases (e.g. *isn't it?*, *don't you think?*). We usually use a personal style in informal letters, everyday conversation, magazine articles, imaginative essays – and even in some kinds of textbook. I'm writing these entries in a personal style, for instance. I *could* have written that last sentence like this: *These entries are being written in a personal style* – but I prefer an informal approach. I think a personal style makes a subject more interesting and easier to understand. Would you agree?

GOVERNMENT WORD WARNING! You'll often find people disagreeing about whether to use a personal or an impersonal style. In school, for instance, one teacher might want you to write an essay on a topic in history or geography in an impersonal way, whereas another might prefer you to use a more personal style. Science reports are usually quite impersonal (but not always) and English essays are usually quite personal (but not always). Try and get a discussion going in class about which general approach to use, for each subject. But keep your head well down. When people disagree about style they can get very uptight!

 voice (in grammar)

inanimate see **animate**

incoherence see **coherence**

indefinite pronoun

PE TEACHER: Right, get into pairs . . . Has everybody found someone? . . . Is there somebody without anyone? . . . Have you no one, James? Oh dear.
JAMES: Never mind, Miss. I'll just sit here and do nothing with nobody.

James and his teacher are obviously getting on very well. Apart from anything else, they have indefinite pronouns in common.

Most pronouns are definite in their meaning: *I* refers very specifically to the speaker; *yours* refers to the listener; *that* refers to an object some distance away; *which* refers to a particular choice; *herself* refers to a specific person; and so on. But there are a few pronouns which are by no means specific. They refer to things in a very general way. Pronouns of this kind are called **indefinite pronouns**. The chief ones are *some*, *any*, *all*, and *none*, and the 12 compound words which you can make using *every-*, *some-*, *any-*, and *no-* with *-thing*, *-body*, and *-one*. (Yes, definitely 12: 3 × 4. Try every combination, and you'll see.)

That's everything, I think, apart from three more examples. Has anyone got anything to say? None of you? Splendid.

pronoun

indicative (in-**di**-kuh-tiv) [ɪnˈdɪkətɪv]

It's one of those interview scenes, like at the end of an Agatha Christie murder story, when the inspector is sorting everyone out.

LADY QUERULOUS: Where was Mary all this time?
INSPECTOR: She stayed in bed.
LADY QUERULOUS: But if she was in the house at the time, she can't have killed Brian.

Question for forensic grammarians: Is Lady Q agreeing that Mary was in the house? Yes. *If* has the same sort of meaning here as 'because'. Now read on.

LADY QUERULOUS: So the murderer must be still outside – in the garden.
INSPECTOR: That is correct.
LADY QUERULOUS: Mary is in great danger. Where is she?
INSPECTOR: If she were in the house, I'd feel much happier.

Further question for forensic grammarians: Is the Inspector saying that Mary *is* in the house? No. He's not sure. He's saying: I would like her to be in the house, but I have a feeling she isn't.

Now let's put two of the sentences side by side:

If she was in the house (she can't have done it).
If she were in the house (I'd feel much happier).

Do you see how the only difference in the first part is the change

from *was* to *were*. The first sentence is saying it's a fact: Mary is in the house. If you want your sentence to express a fact, you put it in the **indicative** mood – the sentence then 'indicates' or tells you that something is so. The second sentence doesn't do this: it says 'maybe'. Sentences which express doubt, possibility, and other such uncertainties are in a different mood (see the entry on **subjunctive** for more about this). Most sentences you speak and write are in the indicative mood. When you say that something's happening, or someone's doing something, or something has a certain quality, you're stating facts, and the verbs you use are all in the indicative. So, next time someone asks you 'What sort of a mood are you in?', you can tell them 'indicative', and you'll probably be right.

 mood   imperative; subjunctive

inference (**in**-fuh-ruhns) [ˈɪnfərəns]
infer (in-**fer**) [ɪnˈfɜː]

PARENTS: We're away at a meeting this weekend. I'm afraid you'll be on your own in the house.
YORICK: I'll be able to have a great party, then.
PARENTS: ?!?

You can fill in the response yourself. It's fairly predictable. Alas, poor Yorick. He has reached the wrong conclusion. He has made the wrong deduction. In a word, he has drawn the wrong **inference**. If you **infer** something, you think that because one thing is true, another thing must be true. Sometimes you're right, and sometimes (as in Yorick's case) you're wrong. Here are some correct inferences (well, usually). If there's smoke, you infer that there must be a fire somewhere. If a noisy class suddenly becomes quiet, you infer that a teacher must have walked in. When you infer something, you ask yourself 'What follows, from what I already know?' In Yorick's case, nothing much, unfortunately.

GOVERNMENT WORD WARNING! Don't mix up *infer* and *imply*. Yorick thought his parents were implying he could have a party. But he was wrong. 'We didn't imply any such thing!', they howled later. *Imply* means to drop a hint, or give a clue, from what's been said. It's something that we can't avoid doing whenever we speak or write. *Inferring*, on the other hand, is something that we do when we listen or read. We have to use our heads to work out what follows from what the speaker or writer has said. So, if what I imply and what you infer turns out to be the same, everyone's happy. But if not, there could be trouble.

informant (in-**faw**-muhnt) [ɪnˈfɔːmənt]

How do you find out about language and how it works? You can:

(a) Sit in a hot bath and think about how other people use language.
(b) Sit in a hot bath and think about how you yourself would use language, if you had the energy.
(c) Sit in a cold bath and wish you were sitting in a hot bath.
(d) Don't sit in any bath, but go out and observe how other people use language.

I would advise trying (a), (b), or (d). But there are problems with (a) and (b). Take (b): just thinking about how *you* speak or write will give you some good ideas, if you're studying English, but it won't give you the whole story. And if you want to study Chinese, say, you can think for as long as you like – it won't help (unless you're Chinese, of course). As for (a), if you try to think about how *other* people speak or write, you can end up in trouble. It's difficult to remember precisely what happens, for a start, and there's a real temptation to make it all up. I have a grammar book at home which says that it's normal English to say 'It is I' and 'That is he'. The author must have been in a hot bath from birth. People just don't talk like that.

How do I know? Because I've been out there. I've listened to what people say, and observed what they write. I've also often asked them for their opinions about language – about what they think words mean, or how they pronounce a word, or whether a particular sentence is well constructed. You can do the same, when you're doing your own language projects. When linguists use people in order to obtain information about the way a language works, they're called **informants** – the people, I mean, not the linguists. If you ever investigate a foreign language for the first time, such as a language from Central Africa or Papua New Guinea, you'll find you have to rely totally on informants. In large-scale studies, the investigator may even have some funds available to pay the informants, because telling someone the facts about your language can take up quite a lot of your time. But I've never heard of an informant who retired with a fortune! (Or a linguist!)

ing-form see **participle**

intensifier (in-**ten**-si-fie-uh) [ɪnˈtensɪfaɪə]

This is going to be a splendidly well-written entry. I'm absolutely certain of it. I'm going to be extremely careful to put an intensifying word or phrase into every sentence. It's awfully tricky, though. When you write sentences like this, they can sound totally artificial, after a while. Incredibly artificial. In fact, I'm hardly able to keep it up. Still, I'm very willing to keep going for a while, for the sake of the entry. An **intensifier**, you'll be gathering by now, is an item which expresses a very high or very low point on a scale of meaning. Virtually all my examples so far have been of words which intensify the meaning in an upwards direction – words like *extremely* and *very*. I've given you scarcely any examples of words which intensify the meaning in a downwards direction, so I'd better make up for this now – words like *hardly* and *scarcely*. I can barely believe it. This entry would be practically useless without them. Here are just a few other examples:

intensifying upwards
utterly, absolutely, in all respects, greatly, a lot, outright

intensifying downwards
almost, rather, sort of, somewhat, only, to some extent, just

By the way, have you noticed that intensifers can be either adjectives or adverbs? That's definitely the truth. That's the definite truth. It's a plain fact. It's plainly a fact. And also that some of them are words and some of them are phrases?

I see I didn't do terribly well, after all. I've just noticed that there are two sentences without any flaming intensifiers in them.

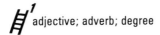 adjective; adverb; degree

International Phonetic Alphabet (fuh-**ne**-tik)
[fəˈnetɪk]

I am about to foretell the future. In about five seconds' time, you will be hunting for an entry beginning with *p*.

This entry will make sense only if you remember exactly what a **phonetic alphabet** is. I use two phonetic alphabets at the top of many entries, to give you some practice in interpreting them. The second one is called the **International Phonetic Alphabet** – or **IPA**, for short. It was devised over 100 years ago, as a way of writing down all the possible sounds of speech. It uses the basic principle of one sound, one symbol, as do all phonetic alphabets, but with IPA the symbols are being used to write down the sounds of French, Chinese, Hindi, and all the other languages. That's why it's called 'international'. Now, there are obviously far more sounds in the languages of the world than turn up in English. So it won't be possible to write down all these sounds simply by respelling English (as I did in the other phonetic alphabet which I've used).

To solve this problem, the IPA has invented several new symbols, some of which look quite weird until you get used to them. For instance, it distinguishes the two *th* sounds of English (as in *thin* and *this*) by using a Greek symbol and an old Germanic one, [θ] and [ð]. The *sh* of English is written with a [ʃ], and the vowel of *see* is written [iː]. The two dots are used to show that this vowel is a long sound (compared, say, with the short vowel of *sit*). Loud syllables are shown with a raised line, not by bold type – so it's ['kiːwiː]. And all IPA transcriptions are given in square brackets. All the vowels and consonants of English are shown in IPA at the front of the book. For now, here's an IPA transcription of the words I used in the entry on **phonetic alphabet**:

see	be	sheaf	seize	brief	kiwi	people	quay	phoenix
[siː	biː	ʃiːf	siːz	briːf	'kiːwi	'piːpl	ki	'fiːniks]

Believe it or not, there used to be a journal for phoneticians where everything was in IPA phonetic transcription. Excellent bedtime reading. Here's an example:

[ðɪs ɪz ə 'sentns 'rɪtn ɪn fə'netɪk 'spelɪŋ.]

How did you find that? (If you're stuck, you can work it out using the list at the front of the book.)

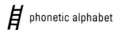 phonetic alphabet

interrogative (in-tuh-**ro**-guh-tiv) [ɪntəˈrogətɪv]

You are being led in chains down a long corridor. You are pushed into a room and made to sit on a chair. A bright light pains your eyes. A man in a white coat stares down at you. You hear. 'Ve haf vays off making you tok, Eenglish peeg.' You wake up.

If you hadn't woken up, you would have been interrogated. White-coat would have started to ask you questions. That's what 'interrogate' means. Like this:

You haf slept vell?
You are goingk to be cooperative?
Are you ready to confess?
Ven vill you realise that resistance iss useless?

Each one of these utterances is a question – you can tell that, of course, because there's a question mark in each case. But notice the difference between the first two questions and the last two. Here are the verb phrases and their subjects (in normal English spelling, this time):

You have slept . . .   Are you ready . . .
You are going . . .   When will you realise . . .

The first two are questions only because of the tone of voice. If I leave out the question marks, I turn them into statements:

You have slept well.
You are going to be cooperative.

But if I leave out the question mark from the last two sentences, you still know they're questions. How do you know? Because there are clear question sentence-markers inside them. In the first case, the word order tells you the sentence is a question (*are you*); in the second case, an actual question-word (*when*) tells you that the sentence is a question (and the word order changes as well, to back it up). A sentence which has clear question markers inside it is called an **interrogative**. These markers could be a question-word at the front (such as *when, why, what*) or just a change in the order of the subject and the verb (such as *are we, do they, will it*).

Two other points. If the question-words do the job of a pronoun, they're called **interrogative pronouns**; examples include *who, which, what, whose,* and *whom*. If these words do the job of an adverb, they're called **interrogative adverbs**; examples include *why, where, when,* and *how*.

Right. Any more questions?

ℍ¹ adverb; pronoun; question   ⌇ declarative; imperative; inversion

85

intonation (in-tuh-**nay**-shn) [ɪntəˈneɪʃn]

How many times have you heard someone say, 'It wasn't *what* he (or she) said; it was the *way* that he (or she) said it'? Lots of times, I expect. What do people mean, when they make such remarks? Let's listen in to a conversation, and see.

John asks Janet whether she'd like to go to the cinema. 'Ye-e-s', she replies, but in a very doubtful tone of voice. 'Well, what does that mean?', asks John, a bit miffed. 'Will you or won't you?'

Because of Janet's doubtful tone, John doesn't know whether the word *yes* means what it says. Said in a definite tone, *yes* means 'yes'.

Said in an uncertain tone, *yes* means – well, 'no', or at least, 'I'm playing hard to get'! Tones of voice of this kind are caused by changing the melody, or **intonation**, of the voice. The 'uncertain' intonation is one of hundreds of tones of voice you can use to express all kinds of emotions – anger, anxiety, excitement, boredom . . .

Intonation can even change the basic meaning of your sentence. Here's a test: see if you can imagine how these sentences sound, then answer the question about them. (The words which stand out in print are to be said in a louder tone than the others.)

John gave a book to *Jim*, and he gave one to *Mary*.

Have you said it correctly, with three beats of rhythm – on *John*, *Jim*, and *Mary*? Right. Now, who gave the book to Mary? You have five seconds to answer.

— — — — —

John, of course. Now try this:

John gave a book to *Jim*, and *he* gave one to *Mary*.

Four beats of rhythm now. So, who gave the book to Mary? Another five seconds?

— — — — —

This time, it was Jim. Putting the emphasis on the word *he*, using intonation, changes the meaning of what you're saying. So it's true, you see. It's not what you say, but the way that you say it.

🧩 stress; tone of voice

intrusive *r* see **linking sound**

inversion (in-**ver**-shn) [ɪnˈvɜːʃn]
invert (in-**vert**) [ɪnˈvɜːt]

If you invert something, you turn it inside out, or upside down, or back to front. You'll come across the notion in all kinds of subjects – maths, music, chemistry, physics . . . – so it shouldn't be too surprising to find it turning up in language studies as well. In grammar, inversion describes what happens when you reverse the order of words in a sentence – especially, a subject and a verb. The usual way of turning a statement into a question in English is through inversion:

Jemima is in the garden. → Is Jemima in the garden?

And you can also get inversion after certain words:

Hardly had I left when the roof fell in.

People don't say:

*Hardly I had left when the roof fell in

– unless they're foreigners or children learning the language. In poetry, though, you'll find all kinds of fascinating inversions, to help achieve a good rhyme or rhythmical effect. Keats uses two in this extract:

Much have I travelled in the realms of gold,
And many goodly states and kingdoms seen.

But in a textbook doubt I that, controlled, such complex inversions there have ever been.

question; statement; subject; verb

IPA see International Phonetic Alphabet

irony (**ie**-ruh-nee) [ˈaɪrəni]
ironic (ie-**ro**-nik) [aɪˈrɒnɪk]

You are out shopping, and pass Fred in the street. Five minutes later, you bump into him in a shop. Five minutes later, you meet him at a bus-stop. You say: 'You're looking well, Fred! Haven't seen you in ages! How've you been keeping?'

Irony, at its simplest, is when you mean one thing, but say the opposite; in order to create a special humorous or dramatic effect. 'Lovely day, again,' you say, when it's pouring. The words and the meaning don't match. We can be ironic just for fun (as in my examples) or to draw attention to a special issue (as when characters speak ironically in a play). Often, the intention is to poke fun at someone or to hurt them – though usually in a fairly mild way. That's the crucial difference between irony and **sarcasm**. When people are being sarcastic, their intention is to ridicule or wound – often to teach a lesson. Sarcasm can be very cruel, often causing a laugh at a person's expense, but often just homing in on a weakness, and hammering away at it. Here's an example I heard once (talking about hammering). A husband had put up a shelf, but as soon as some plates were put on it, it fell down, breaking everything. The wife was heard to say (amongst other things):

That's absolutely brilliant. You're a marvellous handyman. Remind me to recommend you to all my friends.

She was pretty cross. That's sarcasm.

You may have noticed that teachers, just very occasionally, are ironic or sarcastic, at your expense. I know it's unlikely, but say you were late in with your homework, for the third time in a row. You might well receive a comment along the lines of:

Had to do your granny's shopping again, Fortescue?

Whether you call this irony or sarcasm, of course, depends largely on just how pleasant or nasty the teacher means to be.

Incidentally, I used two examples of irony myself, just now, in the paragraph beginning 'You may have noticed'. Did you spot them?

GOVERNMENT WORD WARNING! Irony isn't just a matter of language. Situations can be ironic too. Here's one. You are walking along a school corridor when you see your favourite enemy slip on a banana skin and go crashing down. You howl with laughter, thus failing to see the banana skin which, a few seconds later, sends you crashing down. You may not appreciate the irony, of course.

And when you see a pantomime Dame denying that the baddy is behind her (him), by shouting 'Oh, no he isn't!', that's irony, too. It's called **dramatic irony**, to be precise, when an audience knows something that the characters on stage don't. And does the audience enjoy the joke? Oh, yes it does!

 parody

irregular

The goodest mouses have goed in the bus.

These are not *my* words, I hope you appreciate, but the words of Shula, aged four. Like all other children learning English grammar, Shula has worked out for herself the way you form plural nouns, superlative adjectives, and the past tense of verbs – and she's got it wrong. She thinks that all you have to do is add an -*s* to a noun, an -*est* to an adjective, and an -*ed* to a verb, and you're away. (Incidentally, you don't have to be a child to get this kind of thing wrong. Foreigners learning English also make the same errors.)

It's easy to see where Shula has got her ideas from. Most of the nouns she's come across add -*s* to make a plural, so she assumes that *all* nouns do this. She's heard lots of examples of -*est* being added to an adjective, to express the meaning 'most', so she tries it again here. And she's heard *-ed* used as the ending for the past tense thousands of times, so she assumes that all verbs work in the same way. In a word, she assumes that grammar is **regular**. You and I, however, know it isn't. *We* know that there are lots of **irregular** forms – words and constructions which *don't* follow the usual patterns. There aren't many irregular adjectives in English, but there are a few dozen irregular nouns, and several hundred irregular verbs. Here are some examples. I'll give you a regular case first, then two irregular ones.

A big house. That house is big. That one's bigger. That one's biggest.
A good comic. That comic is good. That one's better. That one's best.
A far off star. That star is far off. That star is further off. That star is furthest off.

One motorbike. Two motorbikes.
One man. Two men.
One knife. Two knives.

I jump. I jumped.
I fly. I flew.
I shake. I shook.

Why not try to build up a complete list of all the irregular words in English?

And the same to you.

 adjective; noun; verb

labial (**lay**-byuhl) [ˈleɪbɪəl]

Labial is the adjective which relates to the word *lip*, when you're talking about speech. Instead of saying 'lip sounds', for sounds involving a noticeable lip movement, you say 'labial sounds'. Labial sounds include [m], [p], [b], [w], and such vowels as [u] and [o]. I think that's all there is to say, really. But look at the entries on **bilabial**, **labio-dental**, and **rounding**, to find out more about the types of sound which use the lips.

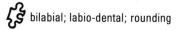 bilabial; labio-dental; rounding

labio-dental (**lay**-byoh **den**-tl) [ˈleɪbɪəʊˈdentl]

Or 'lip-teeth', if you prefer. There are a very few speech sounds you can make by placing one lip near or touching your teeth. In theory, there are two ways of doing it. You can have your bottom lip go towards your top teeth, or your top lip go towards your bottom teeth. In practice, you'll only hear the first of these options. In English, the two chief **labio-dental** consonants are [f], as in *fan*, and [v], as in *van*. If you listen and watch very carefully, you'll often find a labio-dental nasal sound when a [n] is followed by a [f] or [v], as in the word *unfaithful*. And if you're into Dracula, as it were, listen out for a labio-dental hiss when you watch necks time.

Practising their labio-dentals, again, I see

 dental; labial

larynx (**la**-ringks) [ˈlarɪŋks]

Phonetics can sometimes be fun. The task for today is to find your larynx. Put your hand on the front of your throat, and find the bony part which sticks out sharply, called your Adam's apple. If you're not sure that you've found it, swallow hard. The bit that goes up and down is your Adam's apple. And your **larynx** is the part of your throat which lies behind the Adam's apple. The larynx contains your vocal cords, which are housed in a tough casing of muscle and cartilage. That's the reason your throat sticks out so much at that point.

So where's the fun? Well, here's a fact: the Adam's apple sticks out much more in males than in females. Don't take my word for it. Discover it for yourselves. I've known some lovely relationships start that way.

Note to English teachers: It is unwise to let students try to find your larynx by letting them put their hands on your throat.

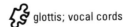 glottis; vocal cords

lateral (**la**-tuh-ruhl) ['latərəl]

This word means 'side' in Latin, and it's used with that kind of meaning in English. In phonetics, it refers to a type of consonant – one where the air passes around the sides of the tongue. You'll remember the name **lateral** if I tell you that lateral sounds are all types of *l* – the word **lateral** begins and ends with *l* – as in *leap*, *look*, *pull*, *fool*, *plan*, and so on. How do you know the air is moving past the sides of the tongue? While you're breathing out, you can't really feel it – but use this trick to help you tell where the air is going. Put your tongue in the position for [l], then – without moving the tongue at all – breathe in sharply. You'll feel the cold air rushing around both sides of the tongue. Easy, eh?

If you live in Wales, you can feel really superior, as you've got an extra lateral sound, compared with English. Everyone's heard of it, because it's the 'double *l*' sound in names like *Llandudno* and *Llangollen* – but not everyone can say it! English people think it's hard to pronounce, but it isn't really. You'll get close enough if you make a normal [l] sound, then – again without moving your tongue at all – turn off the vocal cords. Whisper, in other words. The sound that pops out will be the Welsh *ll* sound.

GOVERNMENT SOUND WARNING! Actually, there are several types of *l* sound in English. Say *leap*, but keep the [l] going for a few seconds. Feel how the tongue bunches up at the top of your mouth,

Hullo, boyo

LLAMA

92

towards the front. Now say *pull*, and keep the [l] going. This time, the tongue is much lower down in the mouth, and the sound is quite muffled in quality. The *l* which comes after vowels in English is often called 'dark *l*', because of this. And the *l* which goes before vowels? 'Clear *l*'.

consonant

lexeme (**lek**-seem) [ˈleksiːm]

Sit down.
Shut up.

Don't worry. I'm not telling anyone off. I just want you to think about the meaning of these two utterances. Notice how *both* words combine to make up the meaning. You can't think of them separately. You don't 'sit' and then 'down', nor do you 'shut' and then 'up'. Each of these utterances is a two-word unit. So, what shall we call the unit? We can't call it a *word*, because we already use that term for each of the two parts. It wouldn't be very clear to say: '*Sit down* is a word which consists of two words'. No, we need a different term, and that's what this entry is all about. A **lexeme** is a basic unit of meaning in a language. Most lexemes are single words: *cat*, *table*, *green*, *jump*. Some are two words, such as *sit down* and *shut up*. Some are three or more, such as *come up with* (meaning 'discover') and *kick the bucket* (meaning 'die'). If you want a list of all the lexemes in a language, you'll find them, neatly listed in alphabetical order, in a dictionary.

This term is also useful when you're talking about the different forms some words can have. Take *go*, *goes*, *going*, *gone*, and *went*, for example. How would you describe this set of words? Even if you don't know the technical terms (e.g. *went* is the 'past tense' form), it's obvious that they are all forms of the one item, *go*. *Go* is the basic unit of meaning: it's a lexeme. And that's what you'll find if you look in a dictionary. All the information will be given in the entry for *go*. If you look up *went*, for instance, the dictionary will tell you to 'see *go*'. Go on. Go see.

dictionary; idiom; vocabulary   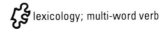lexicology; multi-word verb

lexicography see **lexicology**

lexicology (lek-si-**kol**-uh-jee) [leksɪˈkɒlədʒi]

If you're an '-ologist', you're involved in the study of something. So, *biology* is the study of living things, and *sociology* is the study of society. **Lexicology** is the study of the 'lexicon' – the vocabulary of language. And as there's an awful lot of vocabulary in a language (well over a million words in English), there's a lot to study. **Lexicologists** are interested in such matters as where words come from, how they're used now, how they relate in meaning to each other, and all kinds of other fascinating facts about words.

GOVERNMENT WORD WARNING! Don't mix up a **lexicologist** and a **lexicographer**. Lexicographers don't just study words – they write dictionaries, too. **Lexicography** is the science of dictionary-writing. You can hardly be a good lexicographer, of course, if you don't know about lexicology. But you can spend your whole life as a lexicologist, without ever bothering to write a dictionary. Some people do.

Irrelevant note: There's a famous photograph of three great lexicographers, taken in the early 1900s – Joseph Wright, James Murray, and Walter Skeat. They all have long beards – especially Murray. I wonder if this is because lexicographers get so deeply involved in their dictionaries that they never have time to shave? (Hmm. I've got a beard, too.)

dictionary; thesaurus; vocabulary   lexeme

I think I see a lexicologist gatecrasher...

LEXICOGRAPHERS REUNIO

lingua franca (**ling**-gwuh **frang**-kuh) [ˈlɪŋgwə ˈfraŋkə]

Last week I went to a conference in Brussels. I sat at a table where there was a German, a Swede, a Belgian, and an Italian – and we talked in English. English was the language we all had in common. The Latin for 'common language' is **lingua franca**. English is the world's most widely used lingua franca. But several other languages have an important role as lingua francas, too. French, for example, is widely used in parts of West Africa. German is widely used in Eastern Europe.

Russian is widely used throughout the Soviet Union. Mandarin Chinese is widely used throughout China and in some neighbouring countries. Swahili is widely used in East Africa.

I wonder if there'll ever be a genuine world linguà franca? Many people think that there will be, and that it'll be English. What do you think?

 language

linguistics (ling-**gwis**-tiks) [lɪŋˈgwɪstɪks]

Delete whatever does not apply (and it had better be the 'no' option, or else!):

Any complex subject deserves to be studied carefully, comprehensively, and precisely – that is, scientifically. (yes/no)
Language is a complex subject. (yes/no)
Language should therefore be given a scientific study. (yes/no)

And so it is. The science of language is called **linguistics**, or **linguistic science**. In linguistics, you study the similarities and differences among the languages of the world. What are the essential features of a language? Do all languages have nouns, or prepositions? Do they all have nasal sounds? How much variation is there in a language? Why do people use languages anyway? Why do languages change? Why do children learn to speak so quickly? Why don't I shut up? (Because I'm a linguist, that's why.)

GOVERNMENT WORD WARNING! If you study linguistics, as I've just said, you're a **linguist**. If you speak lots of languages fluently, you're also a **linguist**. The word is ambiguous, therefore. Let's call the student of linguistics 'linguist-A' and the multilingual person 'linguist-B'. You can be a linguist-A without being a linguist-B, or the other way round. I study linguistics, but I don't speak any foreign languages really well (I have enough trouble with English!). And there are lots of people who are good at learning foreign languages who have never studied linguistics in their life.

language

95

linking sound

Turn on Radio 4 and listen to the announcers when they say: 'This is Radio 4.' How do they pronounce the word *four*? It's (faw), [fɔ:]. Next, turn on the radio at 3.59 p.m. (or a.m., if you like, but I wouldn't be that keen, myself), and listen to how they say: 'It's four o'clock.' This time, you'll hear *four* pronounced with an *r* at the end: (fawr uh klok) [fɔ:rəklɒk]. What's going on? The [r] sound is there because the word after *four* begins with a vowel. Speakers with this accent find it easier to run the two words together if they pronounce the *r*, and a [r] which is used like this is called a **linking sound**. Any word which ends with an *r* in the spelling will be pronounced in this way – but there must be a vowel following. Listen to *far off* and *pour out*, for instance.

Now, here's a trickier case. Get a friend to say these sentences quickly:

There are many poor people in Africa and Asia.
John is studying law and sociology.
There used to be a Shah of Persia.

Tape the sentences, if you can, so that you can listen to the result several times. If you can't, get the speaker to say them a few times each, and listen carefully to the words *Africa*, *law*, and *Shah*. Most people put in a short [r] sound at the end of these words, to help link them with the next word, which begins with a vowel. There's no *r* letter in the spelling, this time, and so this kind of linking [r] is called an **intrusive** *r* – the [r] is an 'intruder'. Some people hate the sound of an intrusive *r*. Because it's not there in the spelling, they say, it shouldn't be pronounced at all. But it's a very natural thing to do, and I don't think it'll ever be possible to stop it happening.

 accent    consonant and vowel

lipogram (li-poh-gram) [ˈlɪpəʊgram]

This is one of the weirdest games you can ever play with words (not *the* weirdest: look up **univocalic** if you want to find out about that). The idea of a **lipogram** is to write a sentence – or a story – with one letter of the alphabet missing. Of course, you don't get much credit if you decide to leave out the letter *q*, for instance. I didn't use a *q* in either of my opening sentences. No problem. But try leaving out *t* or s or *a*. Worst of all, try leaving out *e*, which is the most commonly used letter in the language. In 1939, Ernest Wright wrote a 50,000-word novel, *Gadsby*, without a single use of the letter *e*. Here are a few lines from it:

Upon this basis I am going to show you how a bunch of bright young folks did find a champion; a man with boys and girls of his own; a man of so dominating and happy individuality that Youth is drawn to him as is a fly to a sugar bowl.

And so on, for 50,000 words. Try it, and you'll find it isn't so easy. And remember: *the* is banned!

 word games

litotes (lie-**toh**-teez, **lie**-tuh-teez) [laɪˈtəʊtiːz, ˈlaɪtətiːz]

This odd-looking word is so odd that people haven't even decided how to pronounce it yet! Some put the stress on the first syllable, and some on the second. It's got just one meaning, though, however you pronounce it. **Litotes** is a figure of speech where you understate something, in order to emphasise it. It's the opposite of exaggeration (see the entry on **hyperbole**, for more about this). You play something down, deliberately not going on about it – and the result is that you draw particular attention to it. The word comes from Greek, meaning 'simple' or 'meagre' – the idea is that you're saying less than you need to. Here's an example. After a marvellous pop concert, you turn to your friend and say: 'Not bad, eh?' You've used an example of litotes. Now two more:

He's no oil painting. (that is, he's very plain)
She's not exactly in the poor-house. (that is, she's very rich)

By the way, the plural of *litotes* is *litotes* – not **litoteses*, and we don't say **a litote*. Litotes is a not uninteresting way of using language, I think. Or, putting this another way, litotes are extremely interesting.

 figure of speech   hyperbole

low vowel see **close vowel**

major sentence and minor sentence

If you cast your eye over the sentences on this page, you'll find that most of them contain several words, and seem to have quite a lot of 'grammar' inside them. If you were a foreigner, you'd find it was quite difficult to put some of them together. Look at the opening sentence I've just written, for instance. It's got 31 words in it; it's organised into three main parts separated by the commas; and each part is full of nouns, verbs, and all sorts of other grammatical goodies. Each sentence so far in this entry presents a similar picture. Even the fairly short ones would give a foreign learner a problem. Sentences of this kind are sometimes called **major sentences**, because they are formed using the basic grammatical rules of the language.

Now, how much of a problem do you think a foreigner would have with these next sentences?

Yes. Gosh! Mhm. Pardon me! Indiana Jones and the Temple of Doom.

Not much, I imagine. Why not? Because there's not much going on inside these sentences. The long one you would learn off by heart. And the very short ones don't have any grammar to worry about. There's nothing much you can do with *yes*, except say it. Nor do you have much choice with such a sentence as *Pardon me*: you can't change it into a different kind of sentence, by using the language's grammatical rules. You can't say *Pardon you* or *I've just pardoned me*, for instance. Sentences of this kind are called **minor sentences**, because they don't follow the grammatical rules found in the vast majority of other sentences.

↹¹ block language; formula; sentence

malapropism (**mal**-uh-prop-izm) [ˈmaləprɒpɪzm]

In *The Rivals*, an eighteenth-century comedy by Thomas Sheridan, we are introduced to the character of Mrs Malaprop, whose main trait is her mistaken use of long words. Her name is based on the French words *mal à propos*, meaning 'not to the purpose'. Here are some of her comic errors:

Illiterate him, I say, quite from your memory . . . (for *obliterate*)
Sure, if I reprehend anything in this world . . . (for *comprehend*)
He is the very pineapple of politeness . . . (for *pinnacle*)

Now I've explained it, you'll see that these errors aren't as strange as their name suggests. A **malapropism** is simply the wrong use of a long or difficult word. In fact, this kind of error is common whenever people try to use a word they don't fully understand. I expect you've done it yourself, hundreds of times, and been corrected for it often enough by your teachers. However, there comes a point when you get to be so good at language that you just don't make mistakes like that any more. I think I can say, without any fear of constipation, that I've reached that point myself.

¹ spoonerism

mass noun see **count noun**

metalanguage (**me**-tuh-lang-gwij) [ˈmetəlaŋgwɪdʒ]
metalinguistic (me-tuh-ling-**gwis**-tik) [metəlɪŋˈgwɪstɪk]

A **metalanguage** is a language for talking about language. It's the technical term for linguistic technical terms. That's what this book is all about. I am trying to develop your **metalinguistic** awareness. You already know your language. You speak it and write it. Now you have to learn *about* it.

You want more? Read on.

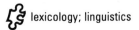 lexicology; linguistics

metonymy (me-**to**-nuh-mee) [meˈtɒnəmi]
metonym (**me**-tuh-nim) [ˈmetənɪm]

CHAZ: Roger's in trouble. He's appearing in front of the bench tomorrow.

BAZ: Why is that a problem? It's only a piece of furniture.

Baz, I hasten to add, is only nine. If he were 19, he would hardly answer like that – unless he wanted to crack a particularly pathetic joke. *The bench* here means 'the magistrates'. Magistrates used to sit along a bench, when they were in court, and over the years the name of the seat came to be used for those sitting on it. Language of this kind is called **metonymy** – a term from Greek, meaning 'name change'. It's a figure of speech where the name of a distinctive characteristic of a thing is used instead of the name of the thing itself. *The bench* is a **metonym**, as is *the crown*, meaning the king or queen. Nicknames are often metonyms, too. If you have a teacher with a long beard, for instance, you might call him *the beard*. And next time someone calls you *big ears* or *four eyes*, take comfort from the fact that you have been labelled with a metonym.

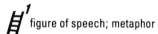
figure of speech; metaphor

mid vowel see **close vowel**

minimal pair

This is not a description of someone with an extremely small pair of spectacles. It is the name you give to a pair of words where just one sound makes the difference in meaning. Here are five **minimal pairs**:

seed	sopping	pence	dental	merry
feed	sobbing	pens	mental	marry

Notice that the ordinary spelling doesn't always show the contrast clearly. You have to say the words aloud, and listen to how they sound. The difference between *pence* and *pens*, for example, is solely in the final sound – as you can see clearly, if I write the two words out in phonetic spelling: [penz], [pens]. The difference between *vessel* and *wrestle* looks even greater, but here too there's only one sound difference between them. The technique of using minimal pairs is an important one, because it's the main way of working out what the important sounds are in a language (see the entry on **phoneme**, for more about them). If you've got a spare five minutes, go through the list of vowels and consonants, at the beginning of this book, and see if you can find minimal pairs for all of them. I'll start you off: *pig, big; bell, tell.* (Actually, it might take you ten minutes – or so.)

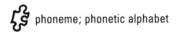 phoneme; phonetic alphabet

minor sentence see **major sentence**

modal verb see **mood**

modify, modification

To 'modify' something is to alter it. If you modify a plan, you change it in some way. You add new ideas. When you modify things in grammar, you also add new ideas. Like this:

ME: Books are fun.
YOU: Tell me more.
ME: Books on language are fun.
YOU: Don't tell me more.

OK. I'll stop there. All I've done is add an extra idea to the noun *books*, using the phrase *on language*. *Books* is the head of the noun phrase (see the entry on **head**, for more about this). It's the most important word in the phrase. *On language* is extra information: it tells you more about the head – what kind of books we're talking about. Any words in a phrase which tell you more about the head are said to **modify** the head. In the present case, the extra words come *after* the head – so we say that they **postmodify** the head (*post* means 'after' in Latin).

You can have the modification going *before* the head, too, and then it's called **premodification** (*pre* means 'before' in Latin). Here's an example:

ME: New books are fun.
YOU: If you say so.

And you can have both premodification and postmodification at the same time:

ME: New books on language are fun.
YOU: You do go on.

Or any number of elements premodifying and postmodifying:

ME: The new, interesting, inexpensive books on language published by Longman with cartoons by McLachlan are holding up my broken chair.
YOU: So they *are* useful, after all.

 phrase   head

mood

She's in a right mood today.

A mood is a state of mind. If you're in a good mood, everything seems fine. If you're in a bad mood, everything seems awful. To know a person's mood is to know how that person is currently looking at the world. And it's the same with language. To know the **mood** of a sentence is to know something about how that sentence is talking about the world.

Some sentences state facts:

That tape costs £3.50.

Some have nothing to do with facts. They give commands:

Do me a favour.

Some ask questions:

Is there a doctor in the house?

Some express doubts, possibilities, uncertainties, wishes, and a whole range of similar meanings.

I might go to the party.
You ought to do your homework first.
If Fred were here . . .

Different sentence patterns (and especially different forms of the verb) are used to express the various moods. In English, the basic pattern of having a subject go before a verb (usually to express a statement) is called the **indicative mood**. A pattern without a subject, used to give commands, is called the **imperative mood**. A pattern which puts the subject after the verb, to ask a question, is often called the **interrogative mood**. And there's also a **subjunctive mood**, which isn't very common in English, that expresses certain kinds of attitude. There are separate entries on each of these in this book, if you can bear it.

By the way, some languages have special verbs whose main job is to express contrasts of mood: they're called **modal verbs**. English has a few, such as *may*, *could*, *shall*, and *must*. They're all auxiliary verbs.

(Remember them? If not, shame on you. You'll have to find a Key Stage 3 book from somewhere, and look up the entry on **auxiliary verb**. Do not pass GO. Do not collect £200.)

⊞¹ auxiliary verb   ⸨ imperative; indicative; interrogative; subjunctive

morpheme see **morphology**

morphology (maw-**fo**-luh-jee) [mɔːˈfɒlədʒi]

When you study the morphology of something, you study its structure. For instance, biologists study the morphology of plants. Geologists study the morphology of rocks. Linguists study the morphology of words. And that's the definition. **Morphology** in language study is the study of the structure of words. It studies how people build up their words, and what job the different parts of a word perform. In English, we can change the meaning of a word by adding prefixes and suffixes:

differ
different
differentiate
differentiation
overdifferentiation

And we can give grammatical information by using special endings:

big	horse	walk
bigger	horses	walks
biggest	horse's	walking
		walked

What shall we call all the basic bits and pieces which are used to build up words? In the examples, you'll find units like *differ*, *big*, *horse*, and *walk*, alongside units like *-ent*, *-ation*, *over-*, *-s*, and *-ing*. To call them 'basic bits and pieces' seems rather crude. We should be able to do better than this. In linguistics, they're called **morphemes** – the smallest building blocks in the grammar of a language. You can use this term, too. No extra charge.

 affix; grammar; inflection; word

multi-word verb

Look at these sentences.
Are you getting by?
Are you looking forward to this entry?
Let me go into this.

Go into what? Into the fact that in each of these sentences, the main verb consists of at least two words, and not the usual one – *look at*, *get by*, *look forward to*, *go into*. You can tell that these words work together as a single verb because you can replace them by a one-word verb:

Look at these sentences. Examine these
    sentences.
Are you getting by? Are you surviving?

And so on. Multi-word verbs are often called **multi-word verbs**, believe it or not – though you'll find that some grammar books call them **phrasal verbs**. They're very common, especially in everyday spoken English. They're very difficult for foreigners to learn, though, mainly because the 'little' words (such as *at*, *by*, and *on*) don't seem to have any clear meaning. *You* shouldn't have had a problem understanding the examples. But I'd better check. How have you got on? Have you caught on? Are you switched on? Should I stop going on?

 verb    lexeme; particle

nasal (**nay**-zl) ['neɪzl]

Pardon me, but I have to get up your nose now. Or, to be more polite, I have to talk about your nasal cavities. They're an important source of speech sounds, you see. In English, there's [m] as in *mix*, [n] as in *no*, and the *ng* sound of *sing*, written [ŋ] in phonetic spelling. If you've studied other languages, you may have come across other kinds of **nasal** consonant – the middle sound in Spanish *mañana* ('tomorrow'), for instance. In French, there are several nasal vowels. So how are nasal sounds made? You make them by lowering the back part of the roof of the mouth – it's called the 'soft palate'. You can see it if you look in a mirror with your mouth wide open: it's the fleshy part which hangs downwards at the back. When you lower the soft palate, the air from the lungs is allowed to go out through your nose, and the result is a nasal sound. You can't feel yourself doing this normally, but if you do a phonetic exercise, you'll get a sense of where the soft palate is, and how it works. Say *ang* ten times quickly, without pausing. I'll wait until you've finished.

There. The flapping movement you felt at the back of your mouth was your soft palate moving up and down. (I advise not doing this exercise during morning assembly, by the way.)

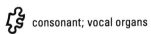 consonant; vocal organs

105

new see **given**

non-count noun see **count noun**
nondefining see **restrictive**
nonfinite see **finite**
nonrestrictive see **restrictive**

onomatopoeia see **sound symbolism**

open vowel see **close vowel**

oracy (**aw**-ruh-see) [ˈɔːrəsi]

Do you have the gift of the gab? Can you talk nineteen to the dozen? These are phrases which mean 'Are you a fast, fluent talker?' If you're not, have you heard about going to kiss the Blarney Stone, at Blarney Castle in southern Ireland? You have to hang upside down to get to it, but if you manage it, you're supposed to come away with the gift of great eloquence! Try it, sometime. Of course, it's not enough being able to talk fluently to your friends in the playground or in the street. The test comes when you have to talk in front of the class, or the whole school, or have to talk to a stranger about a serious subject. Can you be fast and fluent then? Can you keep your thoughts in order, and organise what you want to say so that your message comes across loud and clear? If you're having an argument, can you persuade the other person that you've got a point? If you're explaining how to fix a broken bicycle, do your listeners follow what you're saying? If the answer to all these questions is 'yes', then you really have got some 'oral fluency'. And **oracy** is the term that's been invented to describe people who have the ability to use spoken language in an effective way.

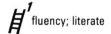
fluency; literate

ordinal numeral see **cardinal numeral**

orthography (aw-**thog**-ruh-fee) [ɔːˈθɒɡrəfi]

The **orthography** is the way the sounds in a language are written down – the letters, and the way the letters combine to make words (the spelling rules). A perfectly regular orthography would have a nice simple system: each sound would have its own letter, and each letter would have its own sound. You wouldn't have to learn any spellings by heart: once you'd learned the letters of the alphabet, and how they sounded, you'd be able to spell anything you wanted. Who said 'Ah, bliss'? Everyone in the English-speaking world, I suspect. It's a sad fact of life that English orthography isn't like this any more. In Anglo-Saxon times, the spelling of English was fairly regular. But over the centuries, the pronunciation has changed many times, and the spelling hasn't kept up. The result is that nowadays we have to remember several rules and many exceptions in order to spell correctly. The irregularities have often attracted the humourist. Here are some lines from one work of art:

I take it you already know
Of tough and bough and cough and
    dough?
Others may stumble, but not you,
On hiccough, thorough, laugh, and
    through . . .

Some people think that the spelling system is so crazy that it should be made more regular in some way – perhaps even totally reformed. In the USA, in the eighteenth century, Noah Webster made a start, but most of his changes (such as *color* for *colour*) are found only in American English. Since then, although several proposals for spelling have been made, none has succeeded. Can you think why?

 phonetic alphabet

oxymoron (ok-si-**maw**-ruhn) [ɒksɪˈmɔːrən]
plural **oxymora**

I like a smuggler. He is the only honest thief.   (Lamb)
O loving hate!   (*Romeo and Juliet*)
The wisest fool in Christendom.   (Henry IV of France, about
    James I of England)
War is Peace. Freedom is Slavery. Ignorance is Strength.
    (Orwell)

These sentences ought to be nonsense, but they're not. Each one has taken two words of opposite meaning, and put them together. The result is to make you stop and think. How *can* there be such a thing as an honest thief? What is Charles Lamb getting at? And, as you think about it, so a possible meaning dawns on you. This use of language is called an **oxymoron** – a figure of speech which brings together apparently contradictory words to make a special effect. It's a strange-looking word, from Greek, where it meant 'pointedly foolish'. You won't only find it in literature, though. Listen around. Have you ever tasted something which was *bitter-sweet* or seen a lazy worker *make haste slowly*? Ever heard a child called a *holy terror* or an *angelic little devil*? Isn't this entry boringly fascinating? (Or fascinatingly boring?)

figure of speech   paradox

palate (**pa**-luht) ['palət]
palatal (**pa**-luh-tl) ['palətl]

Your **palate** is the arched bony structure which forms the roof of your mouth. Run the tip of your tongue over it. Start with the tongue touching just behind your top teeth, then pull it backwards until it won't go any further. Some people can't make it move very far. Others can go quite a way. But be careful! Don't force it too far back, otherwise you might choke yourself! Take a good look at your palate in a mirror. (This is slightly more pleasant than looking at someone else's.) Ignore your fillings, and look at what's around behind the top teeth. Say 'ah', like the doctor makes you do, so that you can see it all. The front part of the roof of the mouth is hard and immobile: it's called the **hard palate**. The back part is fleshy and mobile: it's called the **soft palate**, or **velum** (**vee**-luhm). The soft palate ends in the **uvula** (**yoo**-vyoo-luh), which is the small flap hanging down at the very back of the mouth.

Why is it important to know about the palate? Because the tongue uses the palate to make many speech sounds. Towards the front, English has the [ʃ] sound of *she*, for example. A little further back, there's the [j] of *you*. Further back again, and there's the [k] of *key* and the [g] of *g*. Some accents also have a uvular [r] – a raspy trilled [r] made at the very back of the mouth. If you know French, you've heard that sound quite a bit, I expect. There are several other palatal sounds, too, which you'll hear in foreign languages. And you can move the soft palate up and down, which is how you're able to make nasal sounds, such as the [n] of *nose* (see the entry on **nasal**, for more about them). It's a busy part of the mouth – the busiest, in fact.

GOVERNMENT SPELLING WARNING! The **uvula** makes **uvular** sounds. Don't fall down over your *r'* s.

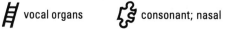

vocal organs   consonant; nasal

paradox (**pa**-ruh-doks) [ˈparədɒks]
paradoxical (pa-ruh-**dok**-si-kl) [parəˈdɒksɪkl]

The richer you get, the poorer you become.

That doesn't seem to make sense. But it must do, mustn't it? People don't go around writing nonsense. Not deliberately, anyway. (The alternative, of course, is that I've finally flipped, and lost all touch with reality. That's ridiculous. Ask any of the parrots sitting on my shoulder, and they'll tell you.) All I've done is used a **paradox** – a statement which seems to be absurd or to contradict itself, but when you look at it carefully, it turns out to contain a truth after all. All that opening sentence is saying is that loadsamoney doesn't make you happy. You end up worrying about it, and get suspicious of other people, in case they take it away from you. You might be rich in cash, but poor in friends, and poor in peace of mind.

The Bible is full of paradoxes. Here are a few from St Matthew's Gospel:

He that findeth his life, shall lose it; and he that loseth his life for my sake shall find it.
Love your enemies.
But many that are first shall be last; and the last shall be first.

109

You'll find paradoxes in everyday life, too. Have you ever heard someone say something like this?

Breaking my leg was the best thing that ever happened to me.

It doesn't make sense, until you learn that the patient married the nurse.

figure of speech   oxymoron

parallelism (**pa**-ruh-lel-izm) ['parǝlelɪzm]

KYLIE: My mum thought I was mad. My best friend thought I'd flipped. The vicar thought I was damned.

I don't know what Kylie has done (murder, perhaps?) to arouse such universal condemnation, but from a grammatical point of view she has to be praised, because she's given me a good example to start this entry. It's an example of structural **parallelism** – a series of structures which are noticeably similar in the way they're made. When you speak or write like this, it can give quite a dramatic lift to what you say, or help you to draw a neat contrast in meaning.

Here's a nice sequence of parallel structures from *Much Ado About Nothing*:

They have committed false report; moreover, they have spoken untruths; secondarily, they are slanders; sixth and lastly, they have belied a lady; thirdly, they have verified unjust things; and to conclude, they are lying knaves.

Parallelism is a good way to begin an entry. And parallelism is a good way to end one.

 free direct speech (if you're puzzled about the murder)

parenthesis (puh-**ren**-thuh-sis) [pəˈrenθəsɪs]
plural **parentheses**
parenthetic (pa-ruhn-**the**-tik) [parənˈθetɪk]

This entry – if you can call it an entry – is going to be about **parentheses**. A parenthesis (another Greek word, meaning 'to insert') is when you insert an extra word or phrase into a sentence in order to clarify something or make a passing remark. Each sentence in this entry contains a parenthesis (as I hope you've spotted). In speech, the melody, loudness, and rhythm of the voice tell you when someone is saying something parenthetic (usually, the voice is quieter and lower). In writing, you should always be able to tell a parenthesis, because its boundaries should be marked by punctuation (usually a pair of brackets (technically called parentheses, by the way), but sometimes dashes or commas). You can even have a parenthesis within a parenthesis, as in the preceding sentence, in fact, but I wouldn't advise doing that too often. If you do (put one parenthesis inside another (as I'm doing now (in order to show you what happens))), and then do it again (as I just did)), it can be very confusing to read. (Agreed?)

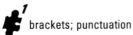 brackets; punctuation

parody (**pa**-ruh-dee) [ˈparədi]
parodist

Are you any good at doing impressions? Good comic impressionists can be very funny. They're able to 'take the mickey' out of someone by mocking the way they speak. Any famous person can be the target – politicians, in particular. What the impressionist does is pick on some noticeable features of the speech, and exaggerate them. If a person has a slight lisp, the impressionist turns it into a huge lisp. If someone has a habit of saying *absolutely*, the impressionist puts it into every sentence – or even two or three times in a sentence.

When you're studying literature, a take-off of this kind is called a **parody** – a recognisable imitation of an author's work in order to poke fun at it or make it appear ridiculous. **Parodists** use exaggeration, just as impressionists do. If an author likes long words, the parodist will make use of *very* long words. If the author likes complex sentences, the parodist will use unbelievably complex sentences. It's extremely difficult to write a parody successfully. You have to know your author very well indeed, and be quite a good writer yourself, to achieve the right balance between slavish imitation and outright distortion. If you go too far one way, your parody will seem just like the original, and the effect would be lost. Go too far the other way, and the parody will seem nothing like the original, and the effect will be lost. If you've read some of these entries, you could have a go at parodying me. I shan't mind.

 irony

parsing (**pah**-zing) [ˈpɑːzɪŋ]

Several times in this book, I've given you a sentence, and shown you how to cut it up into bits. I've also told you the names of the bits, and I hope you'll be able to remember some of them. I did the same in the Key Stage 3 book. What you're doing, when you analyse sentences in this way, is **parsing**. Why do we do it? Well, why do people go to evening classes and learn to take a car engine to bits?

CREEP: To find out how it works, sir.

Exactly. And it's the same with language. When you learn to parse sentences, you learn to understand how they're constructed, what they mean, and how they can be used to best effect. You can begin to explain why one piece of language is more efficient than another. You can spot unclear or ambiguous sentences more quickly. You can talk more precisely about pieces of language which interest you. It doesn't mean that you'll be able to speak more fluently or write better essays – though this *can* happen – any more than learning about car engines will make you a better driver. However, you'll certainly understand more fully how complex language is, and thus be in a better position to say something helpful when you come up against language problems. But beware! It's very easy to do only half the task, when you're parsing sentences. If you cut a sentence up into bits, learn the names of the bits, and then forget to put the bits back together to see what you can *do* with the sentence, you won't get very far. If you did that with a car engine, you'd not get very far either!

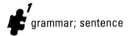
grammar; sentence

participle (**pah**-ti-si-pl, pah-**ti**-si-pl) [ˈpɑːtɪsɪpl, pɑːˈtɪsɪpl]

Emergency! The prisoners are escaping. News Flash! Three of the escaping prisoners have been captured in a hijacked car. The captured prisoners are being brought back to school immediately.

Notice the words *escaping* and *captured*. They're each used in two ways. In the first sentence, *escaping* is used as a verb; in the second sentence, it's used as an adjective. Then, in the second sentence, *captured* is used as a verb, whereas in the third sentence it's used as an adjective. How can this be? How can a word be used in two ways like that? Well, why not? Lots of languages allow this to happen, and there's a special name for the result: a **participle**. The term comes from Latin, meaning 'to share'. A participle is a word which shares some of the characteristics of a verb and some of an adjective.

Look, get this straight! — We are <u>not</u> prisoners who are escaping — We are <u>escaped</u> prisoners, soon to be <u>captured</u> prisoners!

English has two participles. One ends in -*ing*, and is usually called the **-ing participle**. In older grammar books, you'll find it called the **present participle**, but this is rather misleading. The form isn't restricted to present time, but can be used for past and future time as well:

I am watching. I was watching. I'll be watching.

The other doesn't have a single kind of ending, but as the usual ending is -*ed*, it's usually called the **-ed participle**. In older grammar books, you'll find it called the **past participle** – but this, too, is a misleading name, as -*ed* participles are by no means restricted to past time:

The car is parked. The car was parked. The car will be parked.
My watch is broken. My watch was broken. My watch will be broken.

By the way, watch out for the use of the -*ing* participle as a noun:

Smoking is not allowed on the London Underground.

And when participles begin to get boring, stir some life into them by finding ambiguous sentences, based on the differences in the way they're used:

I like shooting stars (I watch them in the night sky).
I like shooting stars (I keep a rifle specially for the purpose).

GOVERNMENT WORD WARNING!
Beware the ambiguity that can appear if you put participles in the wrong place. *Lying all rusty in the garage, Aunt Maude managed to sell her old bike*. Poor Aunt Maude. They should have looked after her better. Brought her in at nights. But of course, it's the bike that's rusty, isn't it? To avoid the ambiguity, the clause beginning with the participle should have gone at the end of the sentence, next to the word *bike*. There's always a risk of ambiguity when you separate a participle from the word it should go with. Separated constructions of this kind are called by various names, but the most popular way of talking is to say that the participle has been left 'dangling'. Of course, there wasn't any real risk of the **dangling participle** causing a misunderstanding in the Aunt Maude sentence, because we know that people don't go rusty. But there are other cases where you wouldn't know what was going on. Try this one: *Staggering drunkenly along the road, Colonel Jones met the vicar*. Who's drunk? So, be careful, especially when you're writing, that you don't make your sentence ambiguous, or cause a laugh when you didn't mean to.

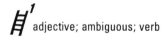 adjective; ambiguous; verb

particle (**pah**-ti-kl) [ˈpɑːtɪkl]

I have not asked Lionel to shut up.

Good for me, whoever Lionel is. But what, you may ask, is the point of that particular sentence? You'll see, if you try to do the following task: name all the parts of speech in that sentence. Off you go.

I? A pronoun.
Have? A verb.
Not? Er – erm.

Asked? A verb.
Lionel? A noun (yes, a proper noun).
To? Er – erm.
Shut? A verb.
Up? Er – erm.

It's the 'er' words I want to talk about. *Not* is an interesting one. No other word in the language behaves in quite this way, turning positive verbs into negative verbs (and having a shortened form, too – *n't*). It's on its own. The same applies to *to* before a verb. It's a different word from the preposition *to* (as in *I went to London*), which means 'to a place'. It doesn't seem to have any meaning at all, in fact – it just marks the verb's basic form (the infinitive form). Again, there isn't another word in the language which behaves quite like this. *Up* is another curious word. It's difficult, at first glance, to know whether it's like a preposition (as in *I went up the hill*) or an adverb (as in *prices have gone up*), or something else. So what shall we call words like these, which seem to be different from the usual parts of speech? Linguists call them **particles**.

adverb; infinitive; negative; parts of speech; preposition

partitive see **quantifier**

passive voice see **voice** (in grammar)

perfect

You are finishing off your latest major work of art – a painting of all the school staff in bathing costumes. You put the last dab of brown on the chemistry teacher's shoe, step back, and say *Perfect*! You mean: it's done, complete, can't be improved upon. *Perfect* often has this meaning of 'complete'. Next time you call someone *a perfect idiot*, you're using the word in this sense – 'a complete idiot'. And this is the sense intended when the word came to be used in grammar books: a **perfect tense** is a form of the verb which expresses a time 'perfectly past'.

Jill has read the new Dai Dastardly book, where he drowns in a vat of tomato soup.
All our family have had chicken pox.

It's all over. She's read it. They've had it. The events are 'perfectly past'. Notice the use of the auxiliary verb *have* or *has*. When you see either of them, you know you're dealing with the perfect.

Unfortunately, the old grammar books didn't tell the whole story, when they described this use of the verb. Look at these next sentences. It's plain that the events are by no means over.

I have lived in Holyhead for several years.
Indiana Jones has been elected our leader.
Fred's been looking for Eliza Dolittle.

Ask the question: 'Is the action or event described by the main verb still applying now?' Do I still live in Holyhead? Is Indiana Jones currently our leader? Is Fred still looking for Eliza Dolittle? The answer is 'yes' to all three. In other words, what the perfect form does is not just tell you about past time; it tells you that an action which began in the past *still* has some relevance for the speaker. It might even be going on now. In the present. It's **present perfect**.

Now that I've told you this, you can perhaps begin to feel the 'relevance' idea in the first two examples in this entry:

Jill has read the new Dai Dastardly book (so she can tell us what happens to him).
All our family have had chicken pox (so they won't get it from the recent outbreak).

The implications of the actions are still with us. And this is what makes the present perfect form of the verb very different from the past tense form. The past tense usually tells you that an action took place at a time in the past which is now over and done with.

I lived in Holyhead for several years (when I was a little boy, but now I live in Bangkok).
Indiana Jones was elected president (in 1888, but he died in 1890).
Fred was looking for Eliza Dolittle (yesterday, but he isn't now).

The perfect form isn't simply a matter of time, therefore. It's more about whether an action is completed or not. Because of this, many linguists these days drop the word 'tense' and call the construction the **perfect aspect** instead. *Has seen*, *have had*, and the others are all instances of the **present perfect aspect**. Got all that? Perfect. But don't go to sleep, because there's a **past perfect aspect** to learn about too (see the entry on **pluperfect** for more about this). Alternatively, do go to sleep, give up grammar, and take up bricklaying.

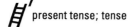 present tense; tense   aspect   pluperfect

personal style see **impersonal style**

pharynx (**fa**-ringks) [ˈfarɪŋks]
pharyngeal (fa-rin-**jee**-uhl) [farɪnˈdʒiːəl]

You have a very important message to tell your friend on the other side of the class. You can't use your normal voice, because that would draw too much attention to the fact that you're not working. So you decide to whisper. But a normal whisper is too gentle, and the sound doesn't carry. You use a stage whisper instead, making it much louder. That carries. Your friend hears the message. Unfortunately, so does the teacher.

You're overdoing the stage whispering, Mr Fortinbras.

You can try to get out of trouble by saying that you were investigating the use of the pharynx in speech (however, I don't guarantee that this will work). The **pharynx** is a part of your throat – to be exact, the part of your windpipe immediately behind your mouth, leading down towards the vocal cords. It's not much used for making speech sounds – though you'll find **pharyngeal** consonants in Arabic, for example. But if you shout out in a stage whisper, the harsh friction which emerges comes partly from the pharynx. Don't do it too much, though, or you'll end up with quite a sore throat.

 vocal organs   larynx

117

phoneme (**foh**-neem) [ˈfəʊniːm]

Here's a game you can play at your next linguistic party. (I hope you are intending to hold such a party. Always have one on 3 February, the feast of St Blaise, who's the patron saint of throats.) You take a word with, say, three sounds in it (sounds, mind, not letters), such as *cat* or *duck*. You then take it in turns to change the word by altering just *one* of the sounds, or adding one sound, so that it makes up a new word. So, *cat* might become *fat* or *scat* or *cab* or *cot*. You mustn't repeat a word, and the game isn't over until you've used *every* vowel and consonant in the language. You can add extra rules, to suit your taste – for instance, no names of people, and no dirty words. (Who said 'Shame!'?) You'll need a list of the vowels and consonants, so that they can be ticked off as people use them. (There's a complete list at the front of this book.)

I don't know whether this game will make your party go with a swing, but it should certainly move your language studies on a bit. Each of the sounds which can cause a change in meaning is called a **phoneme**. Languages have different numbers of phonemes. In the English accent shown in this book there are 20 vowel phonemes and 24 consonant phonemes. Phonemes are like building blocks; you string them together to make words. When you write phonemes down, you put them between slant lines, like this: /p/, /a/, /f/. That way, you can tell the difference between sounds and letters. The written word *sat* has three letters, *s*, *a*, *t* (see the entry on **grapheme** for more about this). The spoken word *sat* has three phonemes, /s/, /a/, /t/. But beware! Not every sound you can make is a phoneme. To find out more about this interesting possibility, you'll have to look up the entry about **allophones**.

GOVERNMENT SOUND WARNING! Notice that, in this entry, and also in the entry on allophones, I've used different brackets from usual – for example, I've written /s/ instead of [s]. This isn't a mistake. Always use square brackets when you're talking about the actual sounds you make with your vocal organs – when you're thinking of them just as sounds, regardless of the language which uses them. But when you're talking about phonemes, you're always talking about a particular language, and thinking of how changes in the sounds make the words change their meanings, as in the party game. You should use the slant brackets when you need to draw attention to this different point of view.

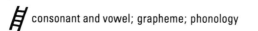 consonant and vowel; grapheme; phonology   allophone

phonetic alphabet (fuh-**ne**-tik) [fəˈnetɪk]

Throughout this book, at the top of many of the entries, you'll find the headword spelled out again in two strange-looking ways. What's going on? They're guides to pronunciation. There's no point in learning a new term if you don't know how to pronounce it. So, in cases where I think you could do with some help, I respell the words – *phonetic*, in this entry, for instance. (I've not bothered to do *alphabet*. I assume that by now you know how *alphabet* is pronounced. If you don't, you've got real problems, man.)

When you write a word to show exactly how it should be pronounced, you use a **phonetic alphabet**, and make a **phonetic transcription**. A phonetic alphabet works on the principle that there should be one symbol, and one symbol only, for each sound. So, for example, the person inventing the alphabet might decide to use the symbol *e* for the sound of the vowel in *set*, and for no other sound. Every time you see that symbol, in that alphabet, you know which sound it refers to; and every time you hear that sound, you know which symbol to use, in order to write it down. English desperately needs this kind of help, because its normal spelling system is so irregular (see the entry on **orthography** for more about this). Look at the following list, for example:

see, be, sheaf, seize, brief, kiwi, people, quay, phoenix

The same vowel sound turns up in each of these words. So, if we're going to write this vowel down in a phonetic alphabet, which symbol should we use? It's very important, now, to realise that there's no single magic way of doing this. You could use any symbol you like – as long as you stick to it afterwards, and don't use the same symbol for any other sound. Obviously, you'll try to use a symbol that reminds you of the sound as much as possible. I wouldn't write this sound down using a *g* or a *u*, for instance – that would be most confusing. In this book, I use *ee* for it. Along with the other symbols I've chosen, my list of words will look like this:

(see, bee, sheef, seez, breef, **kee**wee, **pee**pl, kee, **fee**niks)

Notice how I've put the words in brackets, to show that they're written in a special alphabet. If I didn't, you might think *bee* was the buzzing insect instead of the verb *be*. I've also shown which syllable is the loud one – it's **kee**wee, not kee**wee**, for instance. There's a complete list of all my symbols at the front of the book. I hope you find them an easy way to find the pronunciation of a word you don't know. It shouldn't be too difficult, because I haven't used any strange symbols – only the usual letters of the English alphabet.

The other phonetic alphabet I've used is a different story, because it does use several strange-looking symbols. You can find out what's going on in the entry on **International Phonetic Alphabet**.

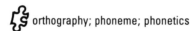 orthography; phoneme; phonetics

phonetics (fuh-**ne**-tiks) [fə'netɪks]
phonetician (foh-nuh-**ti**-shn) [fəʊnə'tɪʃn]

Phonetics is the science of speech sounds. It studies everything that's involved when you speak and when you listen to speech. How do you make sounds with your vocal organs? (What are your vocal organs, anyway?) How do you send sounds to someone else – in other words, how does the air carry sounds? And how do people hear speech sounds? You can see from this summary that the subject has three main branches:

• articulatory phonetics – how sounds are made;

• acoustic phonetics – how sounds are sent;
• auditory phonetics – how sounds are heard;

If you study human speech, you're a **phonetician**. And as most of the language you'll ever meet will be in spoken form (rather than in written form), any serious student of language has *got* to learn about phonetics. That's why all the main technical phonetic terms are in this book.

 phonetic alphabet; phonology; vocal organs

phonology (fuh-**nol**-uh-jee) [fə'nɒlədʒi]
phonologist (fuh-**nol**-uh-jist) [fə'nɒlədʒɪst]

You can make dozens of sounds with your vocal organs, but not all of them are used as speech sounds in English. If you don't believe me, place the tip of your tongue between your lips, press hard on it, then blow. (I advise not doing this while looking at the Head.) The resulting 'raspberry' is not (take it from me) one of the English vowels or consonants. When you investigate the range of sounds which *are* used in English, you're investigating English **phonology**. Phonology is the study of the sound system in a language – or in a group of languages, or (if you're really ambitious) in all languages. (The sound units are often called **phonemes** – there's a separate entry on these.)

Here are some questions a phonologist might ask.
• Do any languages in the world use a raspberry as a consonant? (I don't think so.)
• Do all languages have vowels? (Yes.)
• Do all languages have at least one nasal consonant? (No – though over 95 per cent of them do.)
• Which language has the largest number of speech sounds? Which has the smallest number? (In one recent survey, the largest was a South African language called Xu, with 141 sound units; the smallest was a Pacific language called Rotokas, with only 11 units. Most languages have between 20 and 40 units. English is slightly above average, with 44.)

GOVERNMENT SOUND WARNING! Don't mix up **phonetics** and **phonology**. A phonetician studies the way human speech sounds are made and perceived, regardless of the language they turn up in. If you want to know how the vocal cords work, then all you need is a human being with vocal cords – it doesn't matter which language the person speaks. A phonologist, on the other hand, is specifically interested in the various ways in which languages use sounds. Some phonologists specialise in English, some in French, some in Chinese. Some specialise in small groups of languages. And some try to answer the Really Big Question: are sounds organised in the same basic way in all the languages of the world?

 phoneme; phonetics

phrasal verb see **multi-word verb**

pidgin (**pi**-jin) ['pɪdʒɪn]

Imagine you are a fifteenth-century explorer, looking for the New World. You find it. There are people in it. But they don't speak your language, and you don't speak theirs. You've *got* to talk to them somehow. You need to tell them who you are, and to find out who they are. And there's trade to be done. What will you do?

You'll have a go, of course. You'll probably simplify the way you talk. You won't say, 'Excuse me, I'm terribly sorry to trouble you, but I wonder if I could explain which part of Europe we come from.' Being a typical explorer, you'll say something like: 'We come over sea,' 'You give us food,' 'This big gun – make bang – you no like us, we shoot you dead.' After a few days, and assuming you haven't shot them dead, you'll hear the natives talking. You'll start to pick up some of their words. 'Me like banana,' you might say.

Imagine this kind of dialogue going on over a period of several months. After a while, you'll get into a routine. You'll use the same phrases day after day. The natives will begin to pick up some of your speech. 'Hey, Massa Captain. You want plenty banana?' When you hear them speak like this, you'll be pleased that they're making progress, and you'll start talking back to them in the same way. 'Hey, you boy come see Massa Captain now, chop chop.' This process of copying and half-understanding each other will go on for some time. Eventually, some of the sentences will get quite long. 'Me-you go walk see big-fella lion.' The speech will develop a pattern of its own, with its own grammar, vocabulary, and pronunciation. Everyone in the area will come to talk in the same, simplified way. And in the end, you have a **pidgin language**. Notice that, apart from being very simplified, pidgin is nobody's mother tongue. People just use it when they talk to 'the foreigners'.

Here's an example from one of the best-known pidgins, Tok Pisin of Papua New Guinea, spoken by over a million people. It's taken from a road safety leaflet, and it shows just how advanced a pidgin language can become.

Sapos yu kisim bagarap, kisim namba bilong narapela draiva.
(Suppose you catch-him accident, catch-him number belong other-
  fellow driver.)
'If you have an accident, get the other driver's number.'

This is a long way from 'Me Tarzan. You Jane.'

 creole

plosive (**ploh**-siv) [ˈpləʊsɪv]

Pow! Kabam! Crack! Bop!

This is a learnèd quotation from a Superman comic. Superman, you gather, has caught up with a bunch of baddies, and is letting them have it. As his fists make explosive contact with several chins, these words appear on the page. They're good words. The sounds make you think of the noises as you imagine them to be in real life. You wouldn't get *Soo!*, *Mame!*, or *Loash!*, for instance. That's because there's something special about [p], [b], [t], [d], [k], and [g]. These sounds are short and sharp. They're technically called **plosive** sounds, because there's a mini-explosion of air when you make them. You can actually feel this explosion if you put the back of your hand in front of your mouth while you say *pow*. They're also sometimes called **stop** consonants, because the air from the lungs is stopped short in the mouth as it tries to get out.

That's enough of that. I must get on with my comic – for linguistic purposes, of course.

 consonant   glottis

pluperfect (ploo-**per**-fikt) [pluːˈpɜːfɪkt]

We have elected Indiana Jones as our leader.

This is one of the major events that took place in the entry on **perfect** aspect. But what if the sentence had been written like this:

We had elected Indiana Jones as our leader.

What difference of meaning do you feel? It seems more distant somehow, doesn't it – further removed, in some way. *We have elected* evidently means 'We've just done it, and we've got him as our leader now'. *We had elected* could mean he is no longer our leader:

We had elected Indiana Jones as our leader just before Christmas, but on Christmas Day he fell under a tank, so then we had to elect a new leader.

The use of *had* has the same sort of meaning as *have*, but everything takes place further back in time. Instead of saying *We have just now elected him*, we would have to say *We had just then elected him*. The election was completed much longer ago – just before Christmas, in fact – and the effects lasted until Christmas Day. Then, unfortunately . . .

You can see from these examples that *have* and *had* tell us about whether actions are completed and how long their effects last. They are both instances of **perfect aspect**, therefore. The example with *have* is leading us towards a present time, so it's called the **present perfect**. The example with *had* is leading us towards a past time, so it's called the **past perfect**. In older grammar books, you'll find the term **pluperfect** used for the construction with *had* – from a Latin word meaning 'more than perfect'. And if you've followed this entry, you're more than perfect, too.

 past tense   perfect

polysemic (po-li-**see**-mik) [polɪˈsiːmɪk]
polysemy (po-li-**see**-mee) [polɪˈsiːmi]

This is nothing to do with parrots. The term comes from the Greek words for 'many' and 'sign'. A word which has more than one meaning is said to be **polysemic** (you'll also see the term **polysemous**, in the same sense). I have just opened a dictionary in the middle of the P's, and found two examples straight away:

pip – seed of a fruit; dot on a dice; sign of rank on an army officer
pipe – a musical instrument; a gas pipe; a device for smoking

Many words in the language show polysemy – and the commonest words have the most meanings of all. If you look up a word like *take* in a large dictionary, you'll find that it has well over 20 meanings.

 homonyms

possessive

Tricky one, this. A **possessive** is a word which expresses possession. It's one of the first types of word which young children learn:

Mine.

Then, later, often reluctantly, they learn that there's also *ours*, *yours*, *his*, *hers*, and *theirs*. They're all pronouns, because you can use them in place of a noun phrase. You don't know what the words refer to, until somebody spells them out. And when they do spell them out, they might still use a possessive word, like this:

My car. Your hat. His coat.

The possessive words are now being used as determiners, because they're making the noun more specific – whose car is it, exactly? (See the entry on **determiner**, for more about this.) Notice how possessive determiners are different in form from the possessive pronouns. We don't say **Mine car* – though young children take a while to sort this out.

So, what's tricky? Well, nothing really – except for the point about there being two parts of speech. Maybe I shouldn't begin this entry by saying it's tricky, after all. Perhaps I won't.

 pronoun   determiner

postmodify, premodify see modify

prosody (**pro**-suh-dee) ['prɒsədi]
prosodic (pruh-**so**-dik) [prə'sɒdɪk]

LORD SQUISH: Your grandmother is in the woodshed.
LADY SQUISH: In the woodshed???
LORD SQUISH: In the woodshed.
LADY SQUISH: What is she doing in the woodshed?

If two people acted out this snippet of dialogue, what would you notice about the phrase *in the woodshed*? It would be said in a variety of different tones of voice. The first sentence might be in a matter-of-fact tone – quiet, quite slow, fairly low down in the voice. The second would be much louder and higher in pitch. And so on. These variations in the melody, loudness, speed, and rhythm of the voice are called the **prosody** or (**prosodic features**) of speech. All speech has prosody, in this sense – from the most sophisticated sermon to the most everyday conversation. But beware! When you're studying poetry, you'll find the term **prosody** being used in a much narrower sense, referring to the rhythm of the lines and the rhythmical structure of the verses.

 metre    intonation; stress; suprasegmental feature

quantifier

BILL: The large marbles have rolled down the drain.
BEN: How many?
BILL: All of them.
BEN: Every one?
BILL: Most, anyway.
BEN: You've still got some left?
BILL: A few.
BEN: Are you happy?
BILL: Not a lot.

Poor Bill has lost his marbles, and Ben is extremely concerned about how many have gone. (Well, he would be – they were his marbles.) So the whole conversation is to do with words which express quantity – the **quantifiers** of the language, such as *all, some, every, much,* and *most.* The dialogue shows several quantifiers being used as pronouns, where they stand in place of a noun phrase. (They all refer back to *marbles,* don't they?) And you'll also find them used inside a noun phrase, as a determiner, often followed by *of – some marbles, each marble, most of the marbles.*

Keep an eye open, too, for other quantifying words. There are some phrases which can be used as quantifiers, such as *a great deal of* and *loads of (loadsamoney).* And there are several nouns which express the meaning of a 'part' of something (they're often called **partitives**). *Bit* and *piece* commonly express the idea of 'one part', but often you have to choose a very specific word to go with a noun. For instance, we can't say **a piece of water;* it has to be *a drop of water.* Nor do we say **a piece of grass,* but *a blade of grass.* Similarly, there are many nouns which express the idea of a 'group' or 'collection' of objects or animals – *a bunch of flowers, a flock of sheep.* You've probably come across some of those. Ever done a test like this? 'Fill the gap: a — of lions.' I'll give you a clue: the answer isn't *lot.*

 pronoun   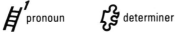 determiner

Received Pronunciation

Most accents tell you where someone is from – Scotland, Liverpool, Australia, the East Midlands, or wherever – but within Britain, there's one accent which doesn't give you any geographical information at all. This accent is called **Received Pronunciation**, and it's usually referred to in short, as **RP**. It's an accent which has long been associated with royalty, government, the law courts, the Church of England, Oxford and Cambridge, the public schools, and the BBC. In the days of the British Empire, it was the accent which travelled around the world. It's called 'received' because it has been passed down by the 'elite' groups in Britain, ever since it developed in the late Middle Ages as the accent favoured by the court and the upper classes. These days, it's spoken by very few people – less than 3 per cent of the population of Britain use it now. Many people have replaced it with a 'mixed' accent – a mix of RP and a regional accent, called 'modified' RP. My own accent is like that – a mix of North Wales, Liverpool, and RP. I say *cup* with a northern 'uh' in the middle, but I say *bath* with an RP 'ah'. However, despite the falling numbers, RP is still the chief prestige accent of the country.

It's the only British accent which is taught to foreigners, for example, and it's still the one you'll hear most often from BBC presenters, judges, bishops, and other members of the country's great institutions. Do *you* use RP? Do any of your teachers?

$\sharp^1$ accent

reflexive pronoun (ri-**flek**-siv) [rɪˈfleksɪv]

Have you ever had your reflexes tested? You sit on a chair, with your legs crossed, and someone taps just below your knee. If the tap lands in the right spot, your leg jerks forwards. That's called a reflex action. The action relates directly to what's just taken place. The term **reflexive** is used in a similar way in grammar. It refers to a pronoun whose meaning relates directly to a previous noun phrase in the same clause – usually the subject. You can always tell a reflexive pronoun in English, because it ends in *-self* or *-selves*.

I saw myself in the mirror – not a pretty sight.
The cats scratched themselves badly.

Notice the difference in meaning between a pronoun which is reflexive and one which isn't:

Mary and John poured themselves another drink.
Mary and John poured them another drink.

In the first sentence, who's getting drunk? Mary and John. In the second sentence, it's someone else.

$\sharp^1$ clause; noun phrase; pronoun; subject

regular see **irregular**

relative (**re**-luh-tiv) [ˈrelətɪv]

We are not talking about uncles and aunts, but we *are* talking about relationships – relationships between the different parts of a

I am your uncle....
I have come from France....
I have written a book....
The book I have written is out next week..
Would you like to see a copy of the book
I have written...

sentence, to be exact. Let's begin with a piece of news:

My uncle has written a book. My uncle is in France. My uncle's book is out next week.

Full marks for short sentences. Low marks for telling the story well. It's a curious, disjointed style, isn't it. The three sentences clearly relate to each other closely – indeed, some of the words overlap. But is there a better way of expressing the closeness of this relationship? There is (did you ever doubt it?). It can all be done in a single sentence:

My uncle, who's in France, has written a book, which is out next week.

Let's look at the first part of this sentence. The word *who* is a pronoun – it stands in for the noun phrase *my uncle*. Its job is to relate the new idea (he's *in France*) to the one that's already been mentioned (the uncle). So it's called a **relative pronoun**, and the clause it introduces is called a **relative clause**. There's another relative pronoun and clause in the second half of the sentence, relating *out next week* to *book*.

129

The chief relative pronouns are *who, whom, whose, which,* and *that.* This sentence, which I'm writing now, shows one of them being used in a relative clause. The sentence that I'm just about to write will show another relative clause. And the one I've just written shows yet another.

YOU: Hang on.
ME: Yes?
YOU: That last sentence hasn't got a relative pronoun in it.
ME: I didn't say it had.
YOU: Oh yes you did.
ME: Oh no I didn't. (See the end of the entry on **irony** for more about this.)

I wrote three relative clauses. The first and second were introduced by a relative pronoun (*which* in the first and *that* in the second). The third left the relative pronoun out – but it's still a relative clause. English lets you do that – but only if there's a subject in the relative clause already.

 clause; pronoun; subordination    antecedent; restrictive

restrictive and nonrestrictive

Here's an example and a question to sort out the linguistic sheep from the goats:

John's just had a letter from his Uncle Eric, who lives in Finland.

This may sound silly, but how many Uncle Erics has John got? I hope you're saying to yourself: 'One – I think – but what on earth is DC getting at now?' I'll tell you in a moment. First, read this example and answer another question:

Maria's just had a letter from her Uncle Eric who lives in Finland.

How many Uncle Erics has Maria got? This time, the answer is, 'More than one – I think.' You'll begin to catch this sense if I carry on like this:

. . . but she hasn't heard from her Uncle Eric who lives in Norway.

If you missed it, that's because you didn't notice the comma, which can make all the difference. So what shall we call this kind of possible difference in meaning?

In the second example, the information about Finland is crucial, isn't it? If you don't hear the bit about Finland, you've no idea which Eric we're talking about. In other words, the meaning of *uncle* has been restricted or defined by what follows. The sentence isn't about 'any old uncle', but about a 'Finland-uncle'. This kind of relative clause is called **restrictive** (or **defining**), because it restricts (or defines) the meaning of the noun.

By contrast, in the other example, you could leave out the clause about Finland and it wouldn't make any real difference. John's had the letter from his Uncle Eric, and that's that. True, the relative clause is giving you some extra information about where he lives, but you don't need to know that in order to work out which Eric we're talking about. The comma tells you: this next bit isn't crucial. In other words, the meaning of *uncle* here hasn't been restricted or defined by what follows – so the clause is called **nonrestrictive** (or **nondefining**).

By the way, you can have restrictive and nonrestrictive meanings in some other parts of the sentence, too. Take a quick look at this:

That's my red car, and that's my green one.

The adjectives here are restrictive, because they are crucial to the identification of the cars. But in this sentence, the adjective is nonrestrictive:

I'd like you to meet my beautiful wife

– unless, of course, there's another wife at home who isn't beautiful!

 relative

rhetorical question (ruh-**to**-ri-kl) [rəˈtɒrɪkl]

My friends, I want to ask you: Where is society going? Where shall we be in a hundred years? Will there still be an England?

Our speaker is warming up for a really strong speech. He's telling the audience his theme by asking a series of questions. But they're not real questions. He doesn't want anyone to answer them. After all, that's what his speech is going to be about. He'll be answering the questions himself. When someone asks a question, just to create a dramatic effect, and doesn't expect an answer, it's called a **rhetorical question**. Of course, just because you're not expecting an answer doesn't mean to say you won't get one. If there's a heckler in the audience, our speaker might well get a response:

Not if you're in charge, mate!

We all use rhetorical questions, don't we? They're common in everyday speech (*Do you think I'm a fool?*). And they're often used in informal writing, too. Would I lie?

 question

roll see **trill**

rounding, rounded

Oooh. Oh. Aw. Whew.

You can be thinking about what might be going on here while I tell you about **rounding**. Rounding means 'lip-rounding'. There are several sounds in English where we noticeably round the lips. The vowel in *soon* [u:] is a good example. Look in a mirror and say *soon* followed by *see* [i:] – you'll see the lips change from **rounded** to **spread**. Several vowels are rounded, as you can see from the opening noises in this entry, and the consonant [w], as in *win*, is rounded too.

Incidentally, you'll sometimes see people speaking in a very 'rounded' style. Watch next time someone talks to a little baby, or to their pet (animal or human). Watch the lips, how they pucker out, for 'lovely lickle baba', and the like. Who's a clever boy, then?

 labial

RP see **Received Pronunciation**

sarcasm see **irony**

semi-vowel see **approximant**

sibilance (**si**-bi-luhns) [ˈsɪbɪləns]
sibilant

ME: Hiss at me. Go on.
YOU: But this entry isn't going to be *that* bad, is it?

No, it isn't (I hope), but hissing is a good way of showing you what **sibilance** means. The best way in fact, because the word comes from Latin, where it means 'hissing'. When you do hiss, you use a [s] sound. And there are three other English consonants which have some hissy features – [z] as in *zoo*, *sh* [ʃ] as in *shoe*, and [ʒ] as in the middle sound of *fusion*. They're called **sibilant** sounds. What causes the hiss? When we make sibilants, we form a narrow groove along the centre of the tongue, and the hiss comes from the air rushing through this groove. Superbly simple.

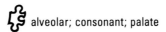 alveolar; consonant; palate

sound symbolism

A single sound doesn't usually have a meaning. It doesn't make sense to ask 'What does [p] mean?' or 'What does [u] mean?' Meaning comes only when you join sounds together to make up words: [p] + [ɪ] + [g] make [pig], and it's the whole word which has a meaning. But sometimes, sounds *do* seem to take on a meaning of their own, and when this happens, we call the effect **sound symbolism** or **onomatopoeia** (o-nuh-ma-tuh-**pee**-uh). Onomatopoeic sounds usually remind us of the noises of the real world. Think about the sounds of these words, while you say them aloud: *splash*, *crack*, *bubble*, *smash*, *woof*, *cuckoo*, and *cough*. Each word refers to a noise of some kind, and the sounds in the word remind us of what the noise is like. But there are some onomatopoeic words which don't refer to noises at all. Think about *blob*, *teeny weeny*, *ooze*, and *slime*. Can you identify the sounds in these words which seem to carry a special meaning? In *slime*, for example, it seems to be the way the word starts with *sl-* which carries an unpleasant 'feel'.

There are lots of English words which start in the same way – *slug, slobber, sloppy, slouch, sly* . . . Can you think of others? When you read a poem, you'll often find sounds which make you think of special meanings in this way.

 alliteration; assonance

spelling reform see **orthography**

spread see **rounding**

spondee see **foot**

stop consonant see **plosive**

stress

Are you suffering from stress, at the moment? All right. Who isn't? But you'll feel better in a moment, when you've finished this entry, because there isn't usually any problem learning about stress in speech. **Stress** refers to the loudness with which you say a word, or a part of a word (see the entry on **syllable** to find out more about this). The loud parts are called **stressed** syllables, and the soft parts are called **unstressed** syllables. You can hear the change between stressed and unstressed syllables if you beat out the rhythm in a line of poetry:

From the waterfall he named her,
Minnehaha, Laughing Water.

This is from Longfellow's poem, *The Song of Hiawatha*. Say the lines aloud, and you can hear the rhythm of the Indian drums in the lines: tum-te, tum-te, tum-te, tum-te. Each 'tum' is a stressed syllable. In everyday speech, of course, the pattern isn't so regular, but there are still several interesting points you should listen out for. In particular, notice how groups of words are related to each other

I'm in stressography....
I study stressographs....
You look stressographic to me...

by a change in the stress pattern. Say these words aloud, for instance. (I'll put the stressed syllable in bold type, as I do when I'm showing the pronunciation of words in this book.)

telegraph – te**le**graphy – tele**graph**ic
photograph – pho**to**graphy – photo**graph**ic

Do you see how the stress changes regularly from one syllable to the next, as the word changes? If I invent a new process, called blogography, you can now tell me how it's pronounced – even though you've never heard it said before. And what does blogography study? Blogographs. You already know how to pronounce that one, too. Isn't this one of the fascinating things about language study? It predicts the future. You already know how to pronounce blogographs, and they haven't even been invented yet.

There. That was, I hope, stress without stress.

⊞ syllable   ⬡ intonation; prosody

subjunctive (suhb-**juhngk**-tiv) [səbˈdʒʌŋktɪv]

We often want to express a difference between something that's a fact and something that isn't. Compare these two examples:

John is in the garden. (FACT. He's there.)
John might be in the garden. He could be. He ought to be. I wish he were. (NOT A FACT. Either he isn't or you don't know.)

A non-fact is something that is tentative, vague, uncertain, possible, doubtful, desirable, and so on. In English, we usually talk about non-facts using the modal verbs (see the entry on **mood** for more about these) – *might, could, can, should,* and the others. But sometimes, we use a special form of the verb, called the **subjunctive**. Some languages use the subjunctive a lot for this purpose – Latin, for example, has a whole set of word endings which express just that sort of meaning. English, by contrast, hardly uses the subjunctive at all. Here's one place where you are going to come across it. You know that in the present tense, the third person singular normally causes the verb to end in -s:

I/you/we/they run. He/she/it runs.

But sometimes you'll see this, especially in a formal style:

We request that the president resign now.

That's the subjunctive form of the verb. No -*s*. The meaning isn't very different from *We request that the president resigns now,* but it does give a little more emphasis to the idea that he 'should' or 'ought to' resign. Also, this use of the subjunctive is more formal in style. And it's much more common in American English, though it seems to be on the increase in Britain.

Here are some other uses of the subjunctive:

I ask that the matter be reconsidered. (as opposed to *is reconsidered*)
If I were ready . . . (as opposed to *If I was ready*)
They insisted that we not leave the house (as opposed to *that we didn't leave*)

And look out for formulaic sentences which use a subjunctive:

God save the Queen. (not *God saves the Queen*)
Heaven forbid! (not *Heaven forbids!*)
Be that as it may! (not *Is that as it may!*)

Suffice it to say that the subjunctive is unusual. Be it noted.

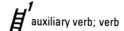 auxiliary verb; verb   mood    imperative; indicative

suprasegmental feature (soo-pruh-seg-**men**-tl)
[suːprəseg'mentl]

Cobblers!

If I wrote this word down in phonetic spelling, it would look something like this: [kɒbləz]. There's one letter for each sound. Six letters – six separate sounds, or **segments**. Now, what *can't* you see in the way I've written the word down? Well, think for a moment about how you'd say *Cobblers!* in real life. It would be fairly forceful – loud, with a descending pitch pattern, and often a raspy tone of voice as well. These are sound effects which apply to the whole of the word. And the same thing would happen if I were to put the word into a sentence:

That's a load of old cobblers!

Now the whole sentence is loud – or at least, it gets louder as you approach the end (a kind of crescendo). You'd say it with a certain rhythmical bounce, too.

All of these sound effects apply to whole syllables, words, and sentences. They don't apply to individual segments. You don't make a loud [k], then a loud [ɒ], then a loud [b], and so on. You simply make a loud word. For this reason, loudness, melody, speed, rhythm, and tone of voice are called the **suprasegmental features** of speech. *Supra-* means 'above and beyond'. Suprasegmental features are sound effects which go above and beyond the individual segments of sound in a sentence. When somebody remarks 'It's not what she said, but the way that she said it,' you can translate this to mean: 'It's not the segments (that is, the words) that she said, but the way that she said them (that is, the suprasegmental features).' What *cobblers* actually means depends very much on how you say it. If you don't believe me, just answer this question. What do you call people who repair shoes?

intonation; prosody; stress; tone of voice

syllable (si-luh-bl) [ˈsiləbl]

Do I need to tell you this in words of one syllable?

If I do, I've already failed, because the word *syllable* has got three syllables in it. The term is from Greek, where it means 'gather together'. What's being gathered together? The vowels and consonants, as you can tell if I break some words up into syllables:

con-so-nant   syl-la-ble   dust-bin

A syllable, as you see, is a part of a word, made up of a combination of vowels and consonants. Quite often, you'll find a syllable made up only of vowels (such as the first syllable of *e-lev-en*) or of a consonant that resounds like a vowel (such as the last syllable of *bottle*, which in speech comes out as [bɒ-tl]). But the vast majority of syllables have both.

You can also think of syllables as part of the rhythm of a word. Each syllable is equal to a 'beat' of rhythm, and the number of beats of rhythm in a word equals the number of syllables. So there are three beats (= three syllables) in *bonanza*. People generally agree how many beats there are, but you can have a row over certain words. Take *million*, for instance. Is this (mi-lee-uhn), with three syllables, or (mil-yuhn), with two? Is *vowel* two syllables or one? I've had to make decisions like this in some of the pronunciations I've given you at the top of my entries. Incidentally, that's where you can find lots of other examples of syllable breaks.

Notice how, when you're writing, it's very important to know where to break a word into syllables. If you reach the end of a line, and there isn't room for the whole of the next word, where will you put the hyphen? If the word's got more than one syllable, you put the hyphen between the syllables. (If there's only one syllable in the word, you don't break the word at all, but take it over to the next line!) Have you learned to do this? If you have, you'll immediately know which to choose in this example:

(1) p- rincess, (2) pr- incess, (3) pri- ncess, (4) prin- cess, (5) princ- ess, (6) prince- ss, (7) princes- s

The only acceptable place is (4). Any other way leaves you with something awkward, misleading, or unpronounceable on one line or the other. Of course, not all words divide so neatly as this, but the principle is the same. Try to make a neat syllable division wherever you can.

consonant and vowel   hyphen   stress

tag question

A **tag question** is very easy to define: it's a sentence with a question 'tagged on' at the end.

This is a tag question, therefore, isn't it?

Notice how the verb changes from positive to negative, as you move from the first part of the sentence to the second. It happens the other way round, too.

The car is in the garage, isn't it?
The car isn't in the garage, is it?

Most tag questions change like this – but you will sometimes get sentences which don't.

So, the car's in the garage, is it?

This means: 'Right, now you're in trouble!'

Notice another thing about tag questions. You can use them to ask someone or to tell someone, depending on your tone of voice.

The film starts at six o'clock, doesn't it? (I'm asking you. I really don't know.)
The film starts at six o'clock, doesn't it! (I'm telling you. In fact, I've told you three times already.)

Tag questions are interesting features of language, aren't they? They can be quite complex, too, can't they? If you use them too often, they become very irritating, don't they? So this had better be my last example, hadn't it?

 question

tautology (taw-**to**-luh-jee) [tɔːˈtɒlədʒi]
tautologous (taw-**to**-luh-guhs) [tɔːˈtɒləgəs]

I myself personally did it.
She sat alone by herself without anyone around.
The cat chased the dog. Also, the dog was chased by the cat.

There is something wrong. Badly wrong. Each example seems to contain unnecessary repetitions. Alone = by herself = without anyone around. You don't need all three. One will do. Unnecessary repetition in language is called **tautology**, and this is something you should really try to avoid, when you speak or write. A certain amount of repetition can be useful – to emphasise something dramatically, for example. A certain amount. But there's no need to repeat yourself, most of the time, to make your point. Such repetition really isn't necessary. You don't have to say things over and over, to get your message across. If you do express points repeatedly, just by changing the words slightly, people will soon realise that you're talking waffle. Reformulating ideas in this way just wastes a lot of space, and wastes people's time. And people don't like to have their time wasted. Time-wasting isn't something that most of us are happy about.

 circumlocution

I myself alone can solve unemployment... Unemployment can be solved by me personally... without any help and only by me can unemployment be solved.......

VOTE WIBLEY – TAUTOLOGY PARTY

text

What does it say in the text, Smythe?
Open your texts at page 1,876.

That's the usual meaning of this word, isn't it? A book, or the printed words in a book. But in language study, **text** has developed a broader sense. It refers to any piece of language which has a definite purpose behind it. It can be written or spoken, and of any size. So, for instance, a poster advertising a disco is a text. A train ticket is a text. A newspaper article is a text. A history book is a text. A sports commentary on the radio is a text. A joke session is a text. A television advertisement is a text. This entry is a text. You can even have a text one word long. Look at some road signs or the signs in large stores. STOP. EXIT. SLOW. It wouldn't take you very long to analyse those texts, I imagine. A poster, or a poem, or a play, would take a little longer. But, whether train ticket or *The Tempest*, the aim is the same: to investigate how language is used in a complete work.

 coherence; cohesion; discourse

tone of voice

Don't look at me in that tone of voice.

That's what Julie said to me the other day. I knew what she meant. The term **tone of voice** is heard so much in everyday conversation that everyone knows what it means – so you can start to play about with it, and use it in jokes. (You couldn't do that with most of the other terms in this book. Don't look at me in that suprasegmental way? Don't look at me with a subjunctive verb? They don't work, somehow.) All I need to do, then, is remind you about what exactly a tone of voice is. It's a noticeable quality which comes into the voice when you want to signal a particular attitude. Your tone of voice can be sarcastic, angry, surprised, puzzled, delighted . . . There are hundreds in any language. And children learn to make a very large number of them before they even get to school. By the time they're into double figures, they know all about tones of voice. I forgot to tell you. Julie was only nine.

 suprasegmental feature

tongue

You don't need a definition of this. If you don't know what a tongue is, there are easier ways of finding out than reading a book on language study. But I do need to tell you what the different parts of the tongue are called, so that you can talk precisely about how speech sounds are made. All the vowels, and most of the consonants, use the tongue, after all. Actually, there's no mystery about it. The terms **front**, **centre**, and **back** are used in their obvious senses, to talk about sounds made with these main parts of the tongue (see the entry on **front** for more about this). The **tip** of the tongue is also an obvious name, for the very front part. In fact, the only unfamiliar term is the name for the part just behind the tip: the **blade**. You can feel the blade being used when you make a [t] or [s] sound. Say [t] ten times quickly, and you'll soon get a sense of where it is.

Well, if you don't know what a tongue is, Muldoon.....

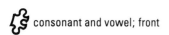 consonant and vowel; front

transcription see **phonetic alphabet**

transformation

Our moggie has just chased next door's Rotweiler out of the garden.
Next door's Rotweiler has just been chased out of the garden by our moggie.
Our moggie hasn't just chased next door's Rotweiler out of the garden.

Well, has she or hasn't she? Who cares (except possibly the Rotweiler)! The point is that you have now seen two grammatical transformations in action. You have a **transformation** when you show that two different kinds of sentence structure clearly relate to each other. The basic structure of the first sentence is 'X has chased Y'. The basic structure of the second sentence is 'Y has been chased by X'. The basic structure of the third sentence is 'X hasn't chased Y'. And if I gave you the basic structure of a fourth sentence ('Y hasn't been chased by X') I'm sure you could work out what the sentence should be. I'm sure you could. (Well, do it, then!)

So, what shall we call these transformations? You can give each one a name, depending on what it does. The switch from the first to the second sentence is a change from an active to a passive sentence (see the entry on **voice** (in grammar) for more about this), so grammarians usually call it the 'passive transformation'. The switch from the second to the third sentence is a change from positive to negative, so it's usually called the 'negative transformation'. Got the idea? If so, see if you can work out what would be involved in a 'question transformation'. All you have to do is turn one of the sentences into a question. 'Has X chased Y?' Exactly.

// negative; question; sentence; statement   *//* voice (in grammar)

trill

You are extremely cold. You shiver. You flap your lips together, making the sound of *Brrrr*. Little children (and sometimes big ones) also make this noise when they imitate a car engine – *brrm brrm*. In speech, when you make a sound by rapidly tapping one vocal organ against another, it's called a **trill**, or a **roll**. The trill at the lips isn't a consonant sound in English, but many English speakers do make a trill with the tip of their tongue. It's called a 'trilled *r*', and you'll hear it a lot in Wales, Scotland, and several other areas. In some French accents, you'll hear a trill at the very back of the throat, using the uvula (a 'uvular *r*'). If you don't normally use a trill in your accent, try to make one – but don't worry if you can't do it. Some people find it very difficult. For them, trilling isn't thrilling.

// consonant   palate; tongue

u

triphthong (**trif**-thong) [ˈtrɪfθɒŋ]

Do you remember what a diphthong is? (If not, you need to look it up now.) Well, a **triphthong** goes one further. It's a vowel which changes its sound *twice*, so that you can hear *three* different qualities. (Tri- means 'three', as in *tricycle*, a cycle with three wheels.) Say the word *higher* as slowly as you can. You begin with the mouth quite wide open, as you would for an *a* sound; then you go for an *ee* sound, and end up with an *uh* sound. There aren't many triphthongs in English, and some accents don't have any. But you'll often hear them in the way some speakers say such words as *lower*, *hour*, and *fire*.

目 consonant and vowel; diphthong

trochee see **foot**

unaspirated see **aspiration**

uncountable noun see **count noun**

univocalic (yoo-ni-voh-**ka**-lik) [juːnɪvəʊˈkalɪk]

This is without doubt the craziest word game that's ever been invented. In a **univocalic**, you have to write a sensible sentence, using as many words as you like, but you're allowed to use only one vowel throughout. It seems an impossible task – but several people have spent ages working on the possibilities. Here is an 'I' poem by a Victorian wordsmith, C C Bombaugh:

Idling, I sit in this mild twilight dim,
Whilst birds, in wild, swift vigils, circling skim.
Light winds in sighing sink, till, rising bright,
Night's Virgin Pilgrim swims in vivid light!

Wow! No soft job for school fools. Cool!

 word games   lipogram

uvula see **palate**

velar (**vee**-luh) [ˈviːlə]

Velar sounds are made by the back part of the tongue against the soft palate (or **velum**). It's not possible to see where this is, as it's too far back in the mouth, and it's not so easy to feel them there, either. But if you say some velar sounds over and over, you'll begin to get a sense of their location. The best ones to use are the three velar sounds in English: the [k] of *king*, the [g] of *get*, and the *ng* [ŋ] sound of *hang*. If you can say Welsh *bach* or Scots *loch*, the *ch* consonant is another velar sound (written [x] in the phonetic alphabet). Oh, and the way most people say *Yukh!*, when they meet something unpleasant, involves the [x] sound, too.

 palate; tongue; vocal organs   consonant; phonetic alphabet

velum see **palate** and **velar**

vocal cords

If I could look down your throat – right down, I mean – what would I see? (I could do it, actually, by using a device called a fibre-optic laryngoscope – a very thin tube with a light inside, through which a picture can be transmitted. You slide the tube up your nose and down the back of your throat, and then you can see everything. Marvellous views. Are you feeling all right?) You'd first see the inside of the nose, then the walls of the throat, the back of the tongue, and the flap which covers the passage to the stomach, when you swallow. Then, way below, you'd see glistening two pale bands of muscular tissue stretching across the throat. They're the **vocal cords** (some books call them the **vocal folds**). When air passes through them, they vibrate, to produce the buzzing sound (known as **voice**) which we use to help make all the vowels and many consonants. If we don't let them vibrate, but just let air pass through them noisily, we make the [h] sound, as in *hot*. We can make several kinds of rough or breathy voices, too, by changing the way in which they vibrate. And when we speak loudly, or change the melody of our speech, it's the vocal cords which are doing the work. The faster we make them vibrate, the higher the pitch of our voice is likely to be. The vocal cords are extremely important in the study of speech, therefore. But don't worry: if you decide to be a phonetician one day, no one is going to shove a laryngoscope up your nose. Not without asking you politely, anyway.

GOVERNMENT SPELLING WARNING! It's **vocal cords** *not* 'chords'. I know you can sing using them, but you can't do several notes at once, like a piano.

♯ glottis; larynx; vocal organs   intonation; phonetics; voice (in phonetics)

vocal organs

This sounds like an easy one. Everybody knows about the vocal organs. All right. Close your eyes and name them – all of them – before you read on.

Did you get: the teeth, the tongue, the palate (not forgetting the uvula), the throat (both the larynx, where the vocal cords are, and the pharynx, which is higher up), the nose, and the lungs? People often forget about the last one – but without the lungs to give you an air supply, you wouldn't make much noise at all.

dental; labial; larynx; nasal; palate; tongue; vocal cords

THE LUNGS, BOY! YOU'VE FORGOTTEN THE LUNGS!

vocative (**vo**-kuh-tiv) [ˈvɒkətɪv]

Lulu, dinner's ready.
My friends, we are gathered here today . . .
I've got a sore wrist, doctor.
Here, you with the glasses, gimme a quid.
Dear Fred . . .

What have Lulu, my friends, the doctor, him with the glasses, and Fred got in common? They're all **vocatives** – a part of a sentence which identifies who you're talking or writing to. You use a vocative when you're calling someone, or just talking to them. I don't use them much in this book, because I don't know who you are. I suppose I could say *all you lot out there*, from time to time. Oh, and *dear readers* might be sweet. But I'm up to letter V, so it's a bit late to do that now. Still, I don't want you to miss out, so I'll finish off with a vocative just this once. Then – as Tom and Jerry say – that's all, folks!

voice (in grammar)

CHEMISTRY TEACHER: William, read out your report of the experiment we did last week.

WILLIAM: Well, sir, we went into the lab, and Joan Brown from 14 Westwood Avenue got some sulphur and picked up a test tube. She was wearing her blue top, and it was about half past ten. I'd had sausages for breakfast. Anyway . . .

That's enough. I imagine the chemistry teacher, like some of his compounds, is about to explode. But why? What's wrong with saying you had sausages for breakfast in your chemistry report? Well, it's got nothing to do with it (I hope you're thinking). What's wrong with saying it was Joan Brown from 14 Westwood Avenue who did the experiment, then? The same. It's irrelevant who actually did the experiment. Whoever mixes sulphur and hydrogen in a certain way will make hydrogen sulphide (and a rotten smell), regardless of whether her name is Joan Brown, or what colour top she's wearing – or what time of day it is, or what anybody had for breakfast. *Who* did the experiment doesn't matter. So – wouldn't it be handy if the English language gave us a way of saying that something happened, without having to say who did it? It might make a chemistry report much more succinct and to the point.

There *is* a way. Look at this:

Joan Brown poured the mixture into the test tube.
The mixture was poured into the test tube.

There we are. I've said what happened, and I haven't had to say who did it. I could, if I wanted, add on who did it:

The mixture was poured into the test tube by Joan Brown.

But I don't have to. Notice, by the way, that the two sentences mean the same thing:

Joan Brown poured the mixture into the test tube.
The mixture was poured into the test tube by Joan Brown.

What shall we call the relationship between pairs of sentences of this kind? Grammarians say that the two sentences are in different **voices**. 'Voice' here doesn't mean anything to do with your vocal organs. It refers to the difference between a 'personal' way of saying something, where the subject of the sentence clearly does the action, and an 'impersonal' way of saying something, where the subject is hidden. The personal way is called the **active voice**, and the impersonal way the **passive voice**. Both types of construction have their place. The passive can be very useful at times:

IRATE DAD: What was that noise?
SMALL BOY: The window's been broken.

Small boy is obviously hoping that the passive will get him out of trouble. He's not saying *who* broke the window. Could have been anybody! Unfortunately, irate dads know about passives, too, so such conversations usually proceed like this:

IRATE DAD: I can see that. Who did it??

Oh dear. Active voice needed now. And an active clip on ear, I suspect.

🪜 verb   **🧩** agent; impersonal style

voice (in phonetics)

Have you ever lost your voice, after a bad cold? Or heard someone who has? It's a very odd sound, isn't it – a kind of harsh whisper. Now, here's a question: what's been lost, exactly? Yes, your voice, I know – but what *is* your voice? To find out, put your thumb and index finger on either side of your Adam's apple. Do not press hard, otherwise you won't be reading the rest of this entry. Say sssss. Do you feel anything happening? Nope. Now say zzzzzz. Ah, that's different. You can feel a dim vibration coming from within the throat, along with the buzzing noise. That's your **voice**. The buzz is caused by your vocal cords vibrating.

When a sound is made using the vibration of the vocal cords, we call it a **voiced** sound. When there's no vibration, we call it a **voiceless** sound. All the vowels are voiced, and quite a few consonants – such as the [m] of *moo* and the [z] of *zoo*. Among the voiceless sounds are the [p] of *pig* and the [s] of *soup*. Check through the list of sounds at the front of this book, and work out which are voiced and which are voiceless. Then work out how many voiced sounds your name has got. (I've got five in David and four in Crystal. Can you beat that?)

🧩 consonant and vowel; vocal organs

vowel see **consonant and vowel**

Entries which appear in the Key Stage 3 book

If you have been looking for a language term in this book, and you haven't found it, it will probably be in the Key Stage 3 book. Here is a list of the terms in that book, to help you check. If the term isn't in either book, sorry! Write and tell me what it is, so that I know. There may be a chance to do something about it, one day.

abbreviation
accent
accents
acronym
acrostic
adjective
adjective phrase
adverb
adverbial
adverb phrase
affirmative
affix / affixation
agreement *see* concord
alphabet
ambiguous / ambiguity
anagram
antonyms / antonymy
apostrophe
appropriate
archaism / archaic
article
audience
auxiliary verb *and* main verb
baby talk
back slang
bilingual
blend
block language
body language *see* communication
borrowing *or* loan word
brackets *or* parentheses
capital letter *see* upper case
case
circumlocution
clause
clause analysis

cliche
clipping
coinage *see* neologism
colloquial speech
colon
comma
command
common noun *see* noun
communication
comparative
complement
compound word
concord
conjunction
connectivity
continuous *see* progressive
contraction
conversation
conversion
coordination
correctness
dash
definite article *see* article
degree
dependent clause *see* subordination
derivation
dialect
dialogue *and* monologue
diction
dictionary
direct object *and* indirect object
direct speech *and* indirect speech
double negative *see* negative
drafting
etymology
euphemism

exclamation
feedback
feminine *see* gender
figure of speech
first language *and* second language
fluency
formal *and* informal
formula
full stop
function word *see* grammatical word
future tense
gender
genitive case *see* case
genre
grammar / grammarian / grammatical
grammatical word *and* lexical word
hyphen
idiom
illiterate *see* literate
imagery
indefinite article *see* article
indentation *or* indention
indirect object *see* direct object
indirect speech *see* direct speech
infinitive
inflection
interjection
intransitive verb *see* transitive verb
inverted commas
irrelevance *see* relevance
jargon
language
lexical word *see* grammatical word
lexicon *see* vocabulary
limerick
literal
literate
loan word *see* borrowing
logogram
lower-case letter *see* upper case
main verb *see* auxiliary verb
masculine *see* gender
metaphor
metre / metrical
monolingual *see* bilingual
monologue *see* dialogue
motherese

mother tongue *see* first language
multilingual *see* bilingual
negative / negation
neologism
neuter *see* gender
non-standard English *see* standard English
nonverbal communication *see* communication
noun
noun phrase
number
object
objective case *see* case
overextension
palindrome
pangram
paragraph
paraphrase
parentheses *see* brackets
parts of speech
past tense
pen name *see* pseudonym
period *see* full stop
periphrasis *see* circumlocution
person
personal pronoun *see* pronoun
personification
phrase
plural *see* number
positive *see* affirmative *and* negative
predicate
prefix *see* affix
preposition
prepositional phrase
present tense
progressive *or* continuous
pronoun
proper noun *and* common noun
proverb
pseudonym
pun
punctuation
question
quotation marks *see* inverted commas
rebus
regional dialect *see* dialect
register *see* variety
relevance